Ancient Egypt

Ancient Egypt

R. Hamilton

This is a Parragon Publishing Book
First published in 2007

Parragon Publishing
Queen Street House
4 Queen Street
Bath, BA1 IHE, UK

For photograph copyrights see page 96
Text © Parragon Books Ltd 2007

Produced by Atlantic Publishing

Cover design by Parragon Publishing

ISBN: 978-1-4054-9188-4
Printed in China

Contents

Introduction   6

Chronology of Ancient Egypt   8

The Pyramids   18

Death, Burial, and the Afterlife   26

Religion and the Gods   34

Temples   42

Agriculture and Food   46

Families and Children   50

Sport and Recreation   52

Crafts and Technology   54

Writing   58

Clothing and Jewelry   62

Trade and the Economy   64

Law and Order   66

Settlements and Housing   67

Military Life, War, and Weaponry   68

The Tombs   70

Tutankhamun   80

The Pharaohs   88

Bibliography   94

Index   95

Acknowledgments   96

Introduction

Egypt was home to one of the earliest and most impressive of the world's ancient civilizations, and also one of the most long-lasting. For much of its approximately 3000-year history, from the time of the country's unification until it was finally conquered by the Roman Empire, this unique society was able to develop its sophisticated culture in relative safety and seclusion, largely protected by the natural barriers of the deserts to the east and west, and by the Mediterranean Sea to the north.

But Egypt did not remain entirely isolated: it traded with neighboring countries and engaged in military campaigns against them, increasing its wealth and territories, and extending its influence beyond its own borders. The country was also settled by a variety of peoples, and the Egyptians not only adopted elements of their cultures, but on more than one occasion were subjected to foreign rule.

The geography of the area was certainly instrumental in Ancient Egypt's longevity, and the River Nile was the key to both its foundation and its survival. The annual floods provided fertile soil and plentiful water for the growth of crops, while the seemingly barren deserts were rich in mineral deposits, including metals, with which the Egyptians learned to make simple tools. These tools enabled them to quarry and shape the huge blocks of limestone and granite that were employed in the construction of their vast statues, temples, and perhaps their greatest legacy, the pyramids.

These tombs stand not only as a testament to the engineering talents of the Egyptians and to the supreme authority of the pharaohs, but also to the strength of belief amongst the people of Egypt in the divine power of their god-kings, whom they relied upon for survival in life, and through whom they could expect salvation in death.

Ancient Egypt was a civilization of extremes, that rose and fell from periods of stability and prosperity, to times of conflict, confusion, and desperation, often in direct relation to the rise and fall of the life-giving Nile. While the moist and fertile Nile Valley preserved that civilization for so long, so too the arid deserts have preserved many of the monuments and artifacts by which we have gained an understanding of that culture today.

Left: Detail of a wall painting from the tomb of Amunherkhepshef, one of Ramesses III's many sons. It shows Ramesses himself confronting the goddess Isis, who is wearing the crown usually associated with the goddess Hathor.

Chronology
of Ancient Egypt

The Predynastic Period
(c. 5500 BC—c. 3100 BC)

Until about 5500 BC, the Nile Valley was inhabited by nomadic hunter-gatherers, who moved from place to place in search of food. However, around this time, people started to settle alongside the Nile in small agricultural communities, taking advantage of the fertile soil deposited by the annual flooding in order to grow crops. They also continued to hunt and fish, began to domesticate livestock such as cattle, pigs, sheep, and goats, and lived in simple houses constructed of mud and straw. Today we usually refer to these early settlers as the Naqada Culture.

There were two main areas of settlement, one concentrated around the Nile Delta in the north, or Lower Egypt, and one in the south, or Upper Egypt; and by about 3400 BC these tribal communities had developed into two distinct monarchies, ruled by kings. Egyptian writing, or hieroglyphics, also developed around this time, probably as a result of Mesopotamian influence, and religious ideas that were shaped by witnessing the natural cycles of the sun and the river were disseminated and assimilated as tribal groups grew and merged. Religious practices at this time already included the placement of funerary goods in graves, and the nobility began to be interred in mastaba tombs.

The latter part of the Predynastic Period, from about 3200 BC, is sometimes known as the Protodynastic Period, and was the time when regions or states, known as nomes, developed and merged, either peacefully or by conquest. Around 3100 BC, Lower Egypt was conquered by Upper Egypt, and unified under one king, probably Menes or Narmer, heralding the start of Dynastic Egypt.

The Early Dynastic Period
(c. 3100 BC—c. 2686 BC 1st & 2nd Dynasties)

The Early Dynastic Period, or Archaic Period, as it is sometimes also known, refers to the time of the first two dynasties of Ancient Egypt, following the unification of the country, which is attributed variously to Menes, Narmer, or Hor-Aha. The Greek historian Manetho records Menes as the first king of a united Egypt, whilst other sources attribute that position to either Narmer or Hor-Aha, and some suggest that they may have been one and the same person. Regardless of exactly who founded the 1st Dynasty, however, it is known that at this time the royal court was established at Memphis, and the main necropolis at Abydos. Throughout the period, the foundations of government, and the bureaucratic structures by which it would operate, were laid. The king was recognized as the "Ruler of the Two Lands," and also as the living embodiment of the god Horus, establishing his absolute and divine power, whilst royal governors were appointed to rule local areas. Hieratic script, a cursive form of hieroglyphic writing, was developed at this time for administrative purposes, and the Egyptian calendar, which was based on the movement of the stars, was also devised.

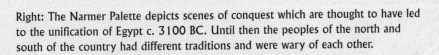

Right: The Narmer Palette depicts scenes of conquest which are thought to have led to the unification of Egypt c. 3100 BC. Until then the peoples of the north and south of the country had different traditions and were wary of each other.

Opposite: Alabaster panel dating from the 5th Dynasty.

The Old Kingdom
(c. 2686 BC—c. 2181 BC 3rd—6th Dynasties)

Also known as "The Pyramid Age," the Old Kingdom marks the first great period of the pharaonic era, a pinnacle of technological and cultural sophistication and achievement, and a time of near continuous stability, which spanned around 500 years. Pyramid building became the most important state activity, developing alongside the belief that the splendor of the king's tomb would guarantee passage to the afterlife, as outlined in the Pyramid Texts. These complex stone structures replaced mastaba tombs for the kings of Egypt, to become lasting monuments to the prosperity of the nation and the power of the pharaohs. The first, the Step Pyramid, was designed by King Djoser's architect Imhotep, and constructed at Saqqara during the 3rd Dynasty, to be followed by the Bent Pyramid, and the first true pyramid, the Red Pyramid, at Dahshur, during the 4th Dynasty reign of King Sneferu. Sneferu's son, Khufu, then oversaw construction of the Great Pyramid at Giza, where Khafra and Menkaure subsequently sited their pyramids. The Great Sphinx was also carved around this time, probably during Khafre's reign. Later, during the 5th Dynasty, the construction of sun temples predominated.

Throughout the 5th Dynasty, the regional governors, or nomarchs, began to increase in power, sparking a degree of civil unrest which was worsened during the 6th Dynasty by an extended period of drought and famine, brought about by a lack of rainfall and thus a lack of flooding in the Nile Valley. By the end of the 6th Dynasty, royal authority has been severely diminished, and following the death of King Pepi II / Peppy II, the nomarchs competed for power, bringing the Old Kingdom to an end and engendering a period of increased instability.

The First Intermediate Period
(c. 2181 BC – c. 2055 BC 7th—11th Dynasties)

The period of decline and disunity that was initiated at the end of the Old Kingdom continued for over 100 years, constituting what is known today as the First Intermediate Period. Famine and internal conflict persisted as local nobles struggled for power. Little is known of the rulers of the 7th and 8th Dynasties, but it is thought that their reigns were brief and their power localized. Some are thought to have continued to rule from Memphis, also contending with Asiatic invasions, whilst nobles in the city of Heracleopolis gained control of Middle Egypt. It was here that Kheti founded the 9th Dynasty around 2160, the kings of which may have briefly regained overall control of the country, but by the 10th Dynasty a rival line, the 11th Dynasty, had been established in Thebes and had gained control of Upper Egypt. Perhaps inevitably, the two powers were engaged in frequent clashes, until the Heracleopolitan kings were defeated, and the 11th Dynasty king Mentuhotep reunited the country, ushering in a new period of order and prosperity.

Perhaps one advantage for ordinary Egyptians that emerged from the chaos, conflict, and weakened pharaonic power during the First Intermediate Period was the rise in the cult of Osiris, and the democratization of funerary beliefs, whereby everyone now believed in a personal judgment at death, independent of the king.

The Middle Kingdom
(c. 2055 BC—c. 1650 BC 11th—14th Dynasties)

Following the reunification of Egypt, the country entered a second period of lasting prosperity and stability that was to bear witness to the flourishing of Egyptian art, literature, and architecture, the strengthening and extension of the country's borders, and also the restoration of pharaonic power.

The 11th Dynasty was brought to an end with the death of Mentuhotep IV, who was succeeded by Amenemhat I, founder of the 12th Dynasty. He established a new capital, Itjtawy, reined in the powers of the local nomarchs, and introduced co-regency in order to smooth the transition between rulers and to forestall future coups. He was murdered, but his son and coregent Senusret I suppressed any further challenge to the throne, and throughout the remainder of the 12th Dynasty, co-regency was to prove highly effective. With increased internal stability, successive pharaohs such as Senusret III turned their focus to regaining lost territories and also to expanding their possessions. Nubia was annexed, and a chain of forts was constructed in order to secure Egypt's borders. Other building projects included magnificent temples at Karnak and Abydos, and pyramids at Dahshur, but the latter were not of the scale or quality of construction of those built during the Old Kingdom. The worship of Amun became increasingly important at this time, but Osiris remained the most pre-eminent of the gods, and the Coffin Texts, which were derived from the Old Kingdom Pyramid Texts, become part of the burial ritual.

With the death of Queen Sobekneferu, who seems not to have had any heirs, the 12th Dynasty was brought to an end, and although it seems that the 13th Dynasty kings managed to maintain their rule over the whole of Egypt until about 1750 BC, it is thought that their reigns were rather short-lived, and symptomatic of a gradual decline that would be emphasized with the establishment of the 14th Dynasty: a line of minor kings that ruled concurrently in the Delta. Meanwhile, a group of foreign kings, the Hyksos, or "Desert Princes," had begun to increase in power in the eastern desert and the Delta, and it was they who would come to establish Egypt's next dynastic line and bring an end to the Middle Kingdom.

Below: The pyramids at Giza, one of the Seven Wonders of the Ancient World. Giza was the most important necropolis for 4th Dynasty Egyptian kings.

The Second Intermediate Period
(c. 1650 BC—c. 1550 BC 15th—17th Dynasties)

It is thought that the Hyksos had been settling in Egypt since at least the latter part of the Middle Kingdom, gradually establishing themselves in positions of power, but it was essentially through warfare and superior weaponry, including the use of horses and chariots, that they managed to gain control of Egypt, marking the first time that Egypt had been subjected to foreign rule, and the start of the Second Intermediate Period.

The Hyksos sacked Memphis and established their capital at Avaris in the Delta, to found the 15th Dynasty, which would endure for around 100 years. The Hyksos ruled as pharaohs, and adopted Egyptian customs, but it seems that their power did not extend throughout Egypt, and the reigns of their kings ran parallel to both the 16th and 17th Dynasties. The 16th Dynasty kings are thought to have been native Egyptians, but almost certainly ruled under sanction of the Hyksos, whereas those of the 17th Dynasty, based in Thebes, declared their independence and retained control over parts of Upper Egypt. Originally a truce seems to have operated between the Hyksos and the Theban kings, but later the Thebans became increasingly rebellious, rising up in a series of campaigns that eventually drove the foreign interlopers from the country.

The New Kingdom
(c. 1550 BC—c. 1069 BC 18th—20th Dynasties)

Spanning almost 500 years, and consisting of three dynasties, the 18th, 19th, and 20th, the New Kingdom is widely recognized as the last great period in the history of Ancient Egypt. It was a time of stability and opulence, when trade, art, and architecture flourished once more, the country's acquisitions and influence increased to their greatest extent and security was assured by the formation of a national standing army. Burial practices also changed with the establishment of a new royal necropolis at Thebes, the Valley of the Kings, which saw the pharaohs' remains interred in deep underground tombs. Although these were largely looted, the discovery of the tomb of Tutankhamun in the early 20th century AD later revealed the prosperity of the period.

Following the expulsion of the Hyksos, King Ahmose I set about strengthening Egypt's borders with a series of military campaigns that set a precedent for many of the New Kingdom rulers, including Tuthmosis I and Tuthmosis III and later Ramesses II and Ramesses III of the 19th and 20th Dynasties respectively. Tuthmosis III is sometimes known as "the Napoleon of Egypt" on account of his military prowess; he not only secured Egypt's borders, but actively extended them to provide the country with a Middle Eastern empire.

As with many of the New Kingdom pharaohs, Tuthmosis III is also well known for his building works, which included several temples to Amun, who rose to prominence to become the most important deity of the period. Yet towards the end of the 18th Dynasty, under the reign of Amenhotep IV, perhaps better known as Akhenaten, the cult of the solar deity the Aten was promoted to the exclusion of all others, and in fact the worship of other gods was briefly proscribed. The traditional pantheon and religious practices were quickly restored during the reign of Tutankhamun, however, and the 19th Dynasty kings Seti I and his son Ramesses II were responsible for great monuments to Amun at Karnak.

Also known as "Ramesses the Great," Ramesses II launched several military campaigns against the Hittites, and eventually secured peace with them, but by the 20th Dynasty, foreign forces, such as the Libyans and "Sea Peoples" were increasing in power, as were the high priests at Thebes. Conversely, pharaonic power was waning, and by the end of the 20th Dynasty Egypt was fragmented once more and the country was in decline.

Above: Fragment of a painted relief from the south wall of the funerary temple of the 11th Dynasty king Mentuhotep II, depicting a jackal raiding a bird's nest.

Opposite below: Detail from the internal wall of the mastaba of Nefermaat at Meidum, where some of the finest examples of 4th Dynasty tomb paintings were discovered.

The Third Intermediate Period
(c. 1069 BC—c. 747 BC 21st—24th Dynasties)

Throughout the dynasties of the Ramesside kings, Egypt became increasingly weak and fractured, and at the dawn of the 21st Dynasty the country was once more divided, with power split between the pharaoh, with his seat at Tanis in the north, and the priests and generals at Thebes in the south. Nevertheless, a degree of unity was maintained by intermarriage between the two lines, and neither challenged the autonomy of the other.

13

When the last pharaoh of the 21st Dynasty, Psusennes II, died in 945 BC, he was succeeded by his son-in-law, Sheshonq I, a powerful general of Libyan origin, who managed to unite Egypt's divided factions by appointing his sons in important positions of power, including Iuput, who was installed as Governor of Upper Egypt, High Priest of Amun at Thebes and chief commander of the armies. Despite Sheshonq I's strong rule, unity was not retained throughout the 22nd Dynasty, and in around 818 BC divisions between the north and south were compounded by the foundation of a breakaway dynasty, the 23rd, in the Delta region itself. This ran concurrently with the second part of the 22nd Dynasty, toward the end of which the 24th Dynasty was also established, and a northern coalition was formed. However, all three dynasties would be brought to an end by invasion from the south, as a series of Nubian kings established their control over Egypt.

The Late Period
(c. 747 BC—c. 332 BC 25th—30th Dynasties)

The Nubians had gained independence from Egypt during the final 20th Dynasty reign of Ramesses XI, and by around 730 BC had grown powerful enough to successfully overthrow a divided and unstable Egypt. The Nubian king, Piy, or Piankhi, moved his forces northwards, finally conquering the Delta princes to establish the 25th Dynasty, which would last for almost 100 years, before another foreign power, Assyria, swept into the country, capturing Memphis in 671 and Thebes in 664 BC. The Assyrians were to rule from their capital, Nineveh, installing the Egyptians Nekau and his son Psamtek, as the kings of Sais and Athribis in the Delta region, marking the beginning of the 26th or Saite Dynasty. Upon Nekau's death, Psamtek was made king of Egypt, and was implored by his Assyrian overlords both to control the dissenting Delta princes and form stronger ties with Thebes. This he duly undertook,

Above: An ornate box, dating from the 18th dynasty, which was used as a container for jars of cosmetics and fragrances. Cosmetics and mirrors were often included in funerary goods, suggesting that adornment was regarded as important in the afterlife.

strengthening and uniting Egypt through a combination of diplomacy and military action, until he was able to wrest power from the Assyrians themselves, and Egypt returned briefly to a period of prosperity and stability.

At the same time, in the east, the Babylonians, Scythians and Persians were also growing in strength, and it was the Persians, led by Cambyses, who next invaded Egypt, founding the 27th Dynasty around 525 BC.

Persian rule lasted for about 120 years, under six kings, and although it seems that some of them attempted to respect Egyptian beliefs and customs, there is no doubt that their rule was resented, and the Egyptians launched several uprisings. Finally, around 404 BC, the Persians were overthrown, and a new dynasty was founded by the Saïte prince Amyrtaeus.

This was the 28th Dynasty, the first of the final three native Egyptian dynasties that would last for a combined total of less than 100 years, but during this time Egypt was once more united and sought to emulate some of the majesty of its ancient heritage. Egypt also strengthened its alliance with Greece, welcoming Greek settlers, and Greek mercenaries into its army. But in 343 BC, the last Egyptian-born pharaoh, Nectanebo II, was defeated by a massive Persian army, led by Artaxerxes III, and the Persians regained control of Egypt.

Below: Vignette from the Book of the Dead showing the deceased engaged in work in the Field of Reeds. Agricultural practices changed very little over time in Ancient Egypt.

The Ptolemaic Period (c. 332 BC—c. 30 BC)

The Second Persian Period was to last for just over ten years, before the king of Macedonia in northern Greece, Alexander the Great, swept the Persians from power in 332 BC and established Greek control over Egypt. Nevertheless, he was seemingly welcomed as a saviour by the Egyptians. Alexander was declared to be a son of Amun, crowned as pharaoh, and established a new capital on the Mediterranean coast, the city of Alexandria. He was also the founder of the Macedonian Dynasty, the first dynasty of what is now commonly referred to as the Ptolemaic Period. Following Alexander's death in 323 BC, rule was passed to his half-brother, Philip Arrhidaeus, and then his son, Alexander IV, after which the Macedonian general Ptolemy proclaimed himself king of Egypt, and founded the Ptolemaic Dynasty; a period of Greek governance that would last for some 275 years. The Ptolemaics ruled as pharaohs, and accepted, if not wholly embraced, many aspects of Egyptian culture, but their influence also began to pervade in many spheres, and Greek was introduced as the official language. During this period, Rome was also growing in power and began to become increasingly involved in Egypt's political affairs.

The last of the Ptolemaic rulers was Queen Cleopatra VII, who ascended to the throne in 51 BC, and briefly reigned alongside her brother Ptolemy XIII until he drove her from Egypt. However, her fortunes were to change in 47 BC, when the Roman general Julius Caesar became ruler of Rome. Having defeated Pompey, who had escaped to Egypt, only to meet his death at the royal court, Caesar arrived there, restored Cleopatra to the throne; her brother, Ptolemy XIII, was drowned. Cleopatra went on to marry her second brother, Ptolemy XIV, but within three years he too was dead, as was Caesar, with whom Cleopatra had by now produced a child, Ptolemy XV Caesarion. In 40 BC, Cleopatra married the Roman consul Mark Antony, and bore him three children, but from 36 BC she ruled as coregent with her son, Ptolemy XV. In Rome, meanwhile, Julius Caesar's heir Octavian, who would later become the Emperor Augustus, had his sights on Egypt. Mark Antony was branded a traitor, and in 31 BC his forces were defeated by Octavian, at Actium off the Greek coast. Antony returned to Egypt, where, in 30 BC, with Octavian's army advancing on Alexandria, he and Cleopatra would both commit suicide.

So it was that on August 31, 30 BC, Egypt succumbed to Roman rule and Octavian was proclaimed pharaoh. The formerly great civilization had finally lost its independence and the country was to become little more than an outpost of the Roman Empire.

Right: Gilt coffin from the Roman Period. The Greco-Roman Period followed on from the Ptolemaic Period until AD 641 when Roman rule ended with a conquest by the Arabs and Islam became the predominant religion.

Right: The Step Pyramid at Saqqara was designed by the celebrated vizier and architect Imhotep and marked the beginning of a millennium during which several such awe-inspiring monuments were built. The Step Pyramid was not just a vast tomb but an entire complex, recreating the city of Memphis for Djoser to preside over in the afterlife.

The Pyramids

The huge stone monuments such as temples and tombs are undoubtedly amongst the Ancient Egyptians' greatest legacies, but perhaps none are more impressive or well known than the pyramids, which were constructed as vast tombs in which to house the mummified bodies of their kings, the pharaohs.

The pyramids are amongst the oldest and largest stone monuments in the world and represent a remarkable feat of engineering, particularly if one considers that they were constructed not with machinery, but by vast numbers of men working with simple wooden, stone, and metal tools.

Pyramid building began during the 3rd Dynasty, which marked the beginning of the Old Kingdom and the "golden age" of pyramid building that would reach a peak with the completion of the Great Pyramid at Giza. As many as eighty pyramids are thought to have been constructed during the time of the Old Kingdom, but as the power of the pharaohs weakened during the 6th Dynasty, the later pyramids suffered a decline in quality, and many have since been reduced to rubble. During the 12th Dynasty of the Middle Kingdom, a revival in pyramid building would take place, but these structures were on a much smaller scale and many also proved to be impermanent. It is thought that the last pyramids were built around 1600 BC.

The First Pyramids

The first pyramid was constructed at Saqqara near Memphis around 2650 BC during the 3rd Dynasty, for the pharaoh Djoser, and was designed by the king's advisor and architect Imhotep. It is a step pyramid and was a development of the first stone tombs, which were known as mastabas. These consisted of a burial pit, over

which a mud-brick platform, or mastaba, was placed. The tomb that Imhotep designed was based on a huge mastaba, upon which five further stone steps were constructed. Beneath this pyramid were several passageways and the burial chamber itself, which was carved in granite. The pyramid was surrounded by stone walls, which enclosed a courtyard containing chapels and other buildings, one of which housed a life-size statue of the pharaoh.

Step pyramids continued to be built until the beginning of the 4th Dynasty and the reign of Sneferu, during which an important development took place. Sneferu oversaw the construction of the first smooth-sided pyramids of which the earliest is known as the Meidum Pyramid, and the second as the Bent Pyramid. The latter was built of much larger blocks than had been used before, and is named because of the change in the angle of its slope partway during its construction. Sneferu's actual final resting place, however, is thought to be the Red Pyramid that was erected near by.

The Pyramids of Giza

The Pyramids at Giza were constructed as tombs for Sneferu's descendants; his son Khufu, grandson Khafra or Khafre, and great-grandson Menkaure (also sometimes known as Cheops, Chephren, and Mycerinus), and they are amongst the most impressive of all the pyramids.

In fact, the Great Pyramid, which was erected during the reign of Khufu, is the largest ever built, being taller than any building on Earth until the 19th century AD, and it still remains the largest stone construction in the world to this day. It is some 480 feet tall, with a base 755 feet square, and it is thought to comprise over two million stone blocks, which range in weight from between two and a half to sixteen and a half tons each, totalling around seven million tons.

Exactly how this huge pyramid was constructed is not known for certain, but the blocks used were obtained by chiselling into the stone at the quarry and driving wooden wedges into these cracks. The wedges were then expanded by pouring water over them to break the stone apart. Next, the blocks would be roughly shaped with dolerite stones, mallets, and chisels, before being dragged to the pyramid site on wooden sleds, which were pulled on ropes by large teams of men. Other slabs, such as those used for the smooth outer casing, are thought to have been mined from farther away and brought to Giza along the Nile on barges, as were huge granite blocks that were quarried far to the south at Aswan. Once at Giza, it is believed that the blocks were dragged into place up huge ramps of earth, rubble, and sand that spiraled around the pyramid. Finally a capstone was placed at the top and an outer casing of hundreds of smooth, white limestone blocks was put in place.

Pyramid Builders

It is likely to have taken over twenty years to complete a pyramid of this size, with a workforce of perhaps 8000 or more men working at the site throughout the year, and although it was once thought that the majority of these men were slaves, it is now recognized that most would have been skilled laborers, quarrymen, and stonemasons,

Opposite above: King Neferikare's pyramid at Abusir, which was the main necropolis for 5th Dynasty kings. The tomb complex of Neferikare, who reigned c. 2475 BC—c. 2455 BC, was intended to be larger than that of his predecessor, Sahure, but it was never finished.

Opposite below: The provenance of the Meidum Pyramid is uncertain. It may have belonged to Huni, the last 3rd Dynasty king, or his son Sneferu, founder of the 4th. One theory is that it was abandoned by Sneferu, whose actual resting place is thought to be the so-called Red Pyramid at Dahshur.

who were assisted during the time of the Nile's flooding by perhaps 10,000 farmers, as a means of paying their taxes. The pyramids were surrounded by other tombs, temples, and palaces, and workmen's towns have also been discovered close to some of the large pyramids and other monuments. These would have housed not only the workers, their families, and officials overseeing construction, but bakers, brewers, and other such craftspeople.

The Pyramids and the Heavens

The pyramids represented a lasting memorial to the power of the pharaohs, in terms both of economic wealth and control over their subjects. However, they were not merely an exhibition of earthly power and riches, nor were they solely safe places in which to house the bodies of the pharaohs and their funerary goods; perhaps most importantly, they emphasized the divine power of the kings. The pyramids were intended as fitting monuments from which the kings would continue to rule in the afterlife, and to which their spirits could return to receive sustenance in the world of the living. Additionally, these structures were not only thought of as tombs, but—as the Egyptian word for them, "mur," reveals—as a "place

of ascension," from which the spirit of the pharaoh could ascend to the stars. This may account for the shape of the pyramids; as a representation of a stairway to the heavens, or as the rays of the sun up which the pharaoh would ascend. The sun god Re was amongst the most important of the gods during the Old Kingdom, and both these ideas are suggested in the Pyramid Texts, but it has also been proposed that the pyramid shape may have symbolized the "Divine Emerging Land" that arose from the sea at the dawn of creation.

However, some of the pyramids, including those at Giza, also seem to be linked with the stars in terms of their orientation, with their sides facing exactly due north, south, east, and west, and aligned with the rising of the sun. True north would have been calculated by taking a reading from the Pole Star, using two "bays" or sticks some distance apart, which were aligned with each other and the star. Shafts leading from the King's Chamber within the Great Pyramid also point toward the Pole Star and the constellation of Orion.

Left: The pyramids at Giza. Pyramid construction reached its zenith with the tomb complexes of Khufu, his son Khafra, and his grandson Menkaure. Khafra's pyramid complex is the best preserved of the three, in particular the magnificent valley temple dedicated to him. The apex of Khafra's pyramid retains some of its original Tura limestone casing, most of which was removed from the site in the ninth century for construction work in Cairo.

The Sphinx

Giza is famous not only as the site of Khufu's Great Pyramid and the pyramids of Khafra and Menkaure, but also as the location of the largest ancient statue ever carved in stone: the Great Sphinx. It is carved in the limestone of the Giza plateau, measures some 66 feet in height and around 200 feet in length, and represents a mythological creature with the body of a lion and the head of a man, or, more specifically, the head of a pharaoh, complete with a royal headdress, or nemes. At one time it also sported a ritual false beard, part of which was discovered in the sand during excavations in 1819, and is now housed in the British Museum.

Sphinxes are found at several sacred sites, and are certainly enigmatic figures, but the Great Sphinx in particular, which is known to have been at least partially buried in the sand for much of its history, has long been shrouded in mystery regarding when it was created and whom it might represent. The fact that it bears no inscriptions dating from or relating to the time of its creation has led to much speculation over its age, and some have suggested that it was sculpted long before the pyramids were constructed at Giza; but it is now generally accepted that it dates from the 4th Dynasty, and the time of Pharaoh Khafra, or Chephren, who reigned from 2558 to 2532 BC, and that it most probably bears his likeness.

Although the face of the Great Sphinx has been badly eroded by wind and sand, various facts suggest a connection between Khafra and the Sphinx. The monument is positioned in front of Khafra's pyramid, alongside the causeway that leads from the Nile to his tomb, almost as if it were a guardian and, furthermore, evidence from his temple complex seems to suggest that he directed the most prolific period of statue-making of the Old Kingdom. Another connection may be found in the relationship between Khufu and Khafra and the gods Re and Horus. It is known that Khufu, Khafra's father, was worshiped as Re, and it is likely that Khafra was worshipped as Horus, son of Re. As the Sphinx is thought to be a representation of Horus, it might be assumed then that it is also a representation of Khafra.

Between the front legs of the Sphinx is a large stone tablet or stele, known as the Dream Stele, which tells the story of how, during the 18th Dynasty, the young Prince Thutmose, or Tuthmosis, fell asleep in the shadow of the Great Sphinx while out hunting and dreamed that he would one day be king if he cleared the sand that covered most of the Sphinx. This he did, and in time he became King Tuthmosis IV.

It is thought that the word "sphinx" may be derived from "shesp ankh," meaning "living image," for the Sphinx was part stone, part divine, part man and part beast, and encapsulated the majesty and divinity of the pharaoh who was both king and god.

Death, Burial, and the Afterlife

The Ancient Egyptians believed firmly in an afterlife, and that death was a brief interruption to an existence that continued beyond the grave for eternity, in a world much like that which they inhabited in life. It was thought that the human body was home to three main spirits that were released when a person died. These were the ka, a person's spirit-double or life-force, which was represented by a pair of upstretched arms; the ba, a wandering soul, which was most commonly depicted as a human-headed spirit-bird; and the akh, a kind of ghost that was represented by the crested ibis. The latter was deemed to return to the stars at death, but it was thought that the ka and ba depended on

Below: Anubis, the jackal-headed god of embalming and mummification, prepares the body of Sennedjem in its anthropoid coffin.

Opposite: Mummiform inner coffin of Sepi, a 12th Dynasty general. It bears the nemes headcloth and false beard, both associated with kingship, suggesting that Sepi was an important military leader.

the body for survival, and so it came to be believed that the preservation of the body was essential if life was to continue after death.

In Predynastic times, most people were buried in shallow graves directly in the sand, which dried the body, leaving many corpses very well preserved. The fact that not all bodies decayed may have contributed to the idea of an afterlife, although as people buried in this way were often accompanied by funerary goods such as tools and pots, it suggests that even at this time there was already a belief in life after death.

Osiris and Eternal Life

The first story concerned with death and rebirth in Egyptian religion is that of Osiris. The Ancient Egyptians believed that their gods had originally ruled on Earth before them, and that Osiris, one of the first kings of Egypt, had been killed by his treacherous brother Set, and his body cut into pieces and scattered. However, his wife and sister, Isis, recovered the pieces and was shown by Anubis how to bind him together with

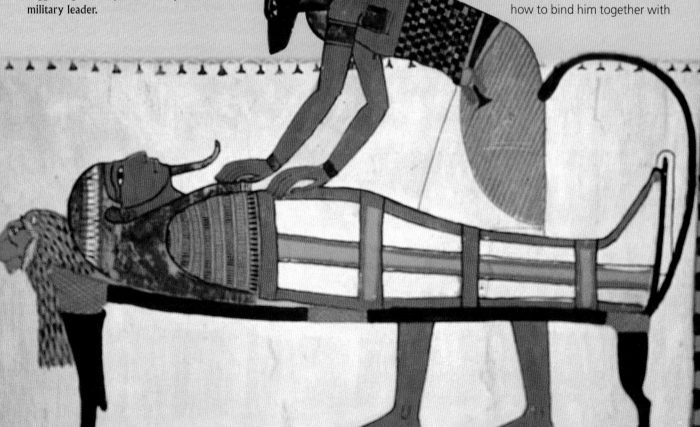

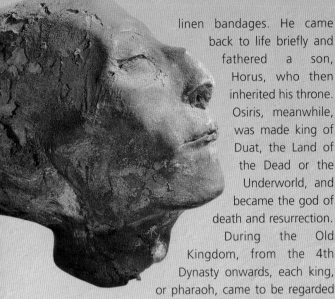

linen bandages. He came back to life briefly and fathered a son, Horus, who then inherited his throne. Osiris, meanwhile, was made king of Duat, the Land of the Dead or the Underworld, and became the god of death and resurrection.

During the Old Kingdom, from the 4th Dynasty onwards, each king, or pharaoh, came to be regarded as the living embodiment of the god Horus, who would become one with Osiris at death, to return to spend eternal life with the gods. This was set out in the "Pyramid Texts" of the Old Kingdom, when it was believed that only the pharaoh would automatically enjoy this particular privilege, but over time, mainly as a result of the influence of Senusret I, during the 12th Dynasty of the Middle Kingdom, the idea developed that every individual would be immortalized through Osiris.

This cult of Osiris promoted the belief that all the people of Egypt would share in eternal life in the "Field of Reeds," an idealized kingdom of eternal spring, but in practice it seems that the idea was first extended to the nobility, as is seen in the "Coffin Texts" of the Middle Kingdom, which were placed within the coffins of important or wealthy people, and later, in the New Kingdom, as extracts from the "Book of the Dead" came to be placed in even the poorest people's graves. These practices developed alongside a belief in a personal final judgment that provided everyone with an opportunity of entry into the afterlife.

The Last Judgment
(The Weighing of the Heart or The Judgment of Osiris)

Prior to the spread of the belief in a final judgment, acceptance into the afterlife was believed to be guaranteed if a person had conducted their life according to the principles of maat, the Egyptian notion of order and morality, but following a breakdown in order during the First Intermediate Period, the idea was promoted that individuals would actually be judged before the gods by Osiris for their earthly actions.

First, a person had to undertake a perilous journey through the Underworld, accompanied by their ba, in order to reach the Hall of Judgment, where, in front of Osiris and forty-two assistants, they would deny having committed any of a long list of sins, before proceeding to the next stage, the Weighing of the Heart. The jackal-headed Anubis would place their heart on a pair of scales, where it had to balance exactly with the feather of truth, belonging to the goddess Maat. If the heart was heavy with sin, then it would be eaten by Ammut/Ammit, the "Devourer of Souls," a terrifying beast with the head of a crocodile, the forequarters of a lion, and the hindquarters of a hippopotamus. As the heart was believed to contain the "self," a person would then cease to exist, and be denied passage to eternal life. However, if the scales balanced, the individual would be permitted to join Osiris in the afterlife, and his spirit was free to move between the lands of the living and the dead.

Opposite: A scene from Inherkha's tomb at Deir el-Medina. A priest wearing the mask of Anubis proffers a bowl of water to the mummy, part of the Opening of the Mouth ceremony which would restore the deceased's senses in readiness for the afterlife.

Above: Head of Queen Tiye, principal wife of Amenhotep III and mother of the heretic king Akhenaten.

Below: Mummified head of Nebiry, chief of the royal stables during the reign of Tuthmosis III.

Above: Upper part of an anthropomorphic coffin, dating from the beginning of the Late Period, with blackened face, lotus-ornamented wig, and chest ornaments.

Mummification

The Egyptians may have observed the preservative effect that burials in sand had on the body fairly early on, but as coffins and tombs became grander and more permanent places in which to house the dead, new ways had to be found in order to prevent the body from decaying. This resulted in the process of embalming that has become known as "mummification," a word that came from the Arabic "mummiya," or bitumen, in the mistaken belief that some resin-blackened bodies that were discovered in the 19th century AD had been coated in tar. However, these were generally poorly embalmed corpses from the Late Period, when the process had passed its peak, which had simply been filled with resin.

Mummification is thought to have begun around 2600 BC during the early Fourth Dynasty, and continued for some 3000 years until the Coptic Period, but the practice was most widespread during the New Kingdom, by which time the process had also become highly refined and effective.

Despite this, however, the poorest people generally continued to be buried, and indeed embalmed, much more simply, whilst the wealthy could afford more extravagant methods of preservation and places of burial.

The Embalming Process

The Egyptians realized that it was essential to remove the internal organs if decay was to be prevented, and also that a drying agent was required. This they found in the form of natron, a compound of salts that occurred naturally in the desert and particularly around the shores of lakes.

As the place where the sun set and supposedly entered the Underworld, the west was most closely associated with the dead. So, shortly after death, a body would be taken to a place of purification on the Nile's west bank, known as the ibu, where it would be washed in natron solution before being taken to the wabt or per nefer, where the embalming would be performed. The cheapest and most simple method involved emptying the stomach, washing out the body cavity and covering the corpse in natron for forty days. Slightly more costly was to inject a chemical purge into the body, to dissolve the internal organs before the natron treatment, but the best and most expensive method was far more complex.

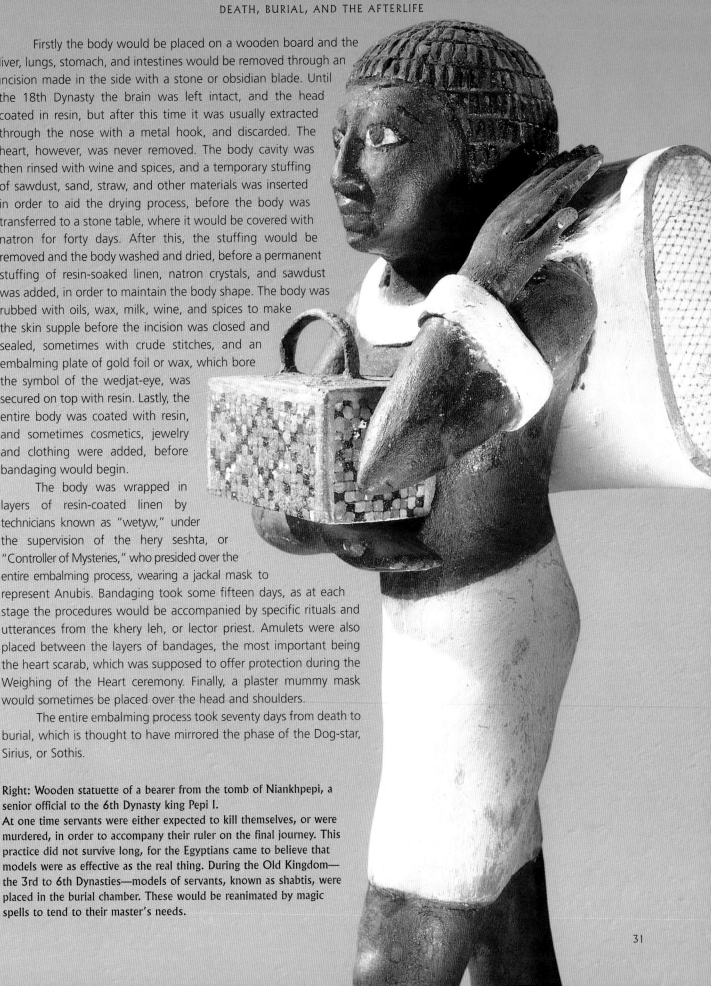

Firstly the body would be placed on a wooden board and the liver, lungs, stomach, and intestines would be removed through an incision made in the side with a stone or obsidian blade. Until the 18th Dynasty the brain was left intact, and the head coated in resin, but after this time it was usually extracted through the nose with a metal hook, and discarded. The heart, however, was never removed. The body cavity was then rinsed with wine and spices, and a temporary stuffing of sawdust, sand, straw, and other materials was inserted in order to aid the drying process, before the body was transferred to a stone table, where it would be covered with natron for forty days. After this, the stuffing would be removed and the body washed and dried, before a permanent stuffing of resin-soaked linen, natron crystals, and sawdust was added, in order to maintain the body shape. The body was rubbed with oils, wax, milk, wine, and spices to make the skin supple before the incision was closed and sealed, sometimes with crude stitches, and an embalming plate of gold foil or wax, which bore the symbol of the wedjat-eye, was secured on top with resin. Lastly, the entire body was coated with resin, and sometimes cosmetics, jewelry and clothing were added, before bandaging would begin.

The body was wrapped in layers of resin-coated linen by technicians known as "wetyw," under the supervision of the hery seshta, or "Controller of Mysteries," who presided over the entire embalming process, wearing a jackal mask to represent Anubis. Bandaging took some fifteen days, as at each stage the procedures would be accompanied by specific rituals and utterances from the khery leh, or lector priest. Amulets were also placed between the layers of bandages, the most important being the heart scarab, which was supposed to offer protection during the Weighing of the Heart ceremony. Finally, a plaster mummy mask would sometimes be placed over the head and shoulders.

The entire embalming process took seventy days from death to burial, which is thought to have mirrored the phase of the Dog-star, Sirius, or Sothis.

Right: Wooden statuette of a bearer from the tomb of Niankhpepi, a senior official to the 6th Dynasty king Pepi I.
At one time servants were either expected to kill themselves, or were murdered, in order to accompany their ruler on the final journey. This practice did not survive long, for the Egyptians came to believe that models were as effective as the real thing. During the Old Kingdom—the 3rd to 6th Dynasties—models of servants, known as shabtis, were placed in the burial chamber. These would be reanimated by magic spells to tend to their master's needs.

Canopic Jars

Unlike the brain, which was discarded, or the heart, which was left in place, the liver, lungs, stomach, and intestines were all separately embalmed in much the same way as the body. They were dried in natron, anointed with oils, coated with resin, and bandaged in linen parcels. These packages were then placed in their own containers, which we know as canopic jars. These jars were made of wood, stone, or pottery, and were mummiform in shape, and the stoppers were often shaped and painted to represent the head of Osiris. However, from the time of the New Kingdom, the stoppers always represented the heads of the four Sons of Horus: the human-headed Imsety, baboon-headed Hapy, jackal-headed Duamutef, and falcon-headed Qebhsnuef, who looked after the liver, lungs, stomach, and intestines respectively, and are known as the canopic deities. The jars were placed in a wooden or stone chest, and continued to be included amongst funerary goods even when, during the 21st Dynasty, it became the practice to place the linen-packaged organs back into the body, accompanied by small figures of the Sons of Horus.

Funerals and Burial

Once the process of mummification was complete, the body would be placed inside a wooden coffin or mummy case, which may have been ornately carved, painted, and decorated with spells. The coffin of a pharaoh was sometimes put inside several other coffins, and ultimately placed within a stone sarcophagus at burial. The family of the dead would then travel to the west bank of the Nile to carry the body to its final resting place. In the case of nobles and the wealthy, this would be a stone tomb that would often have been lavishly decorated inside with paintings depicting activities enjoyed in life, so that they might be similarly enjoyed in the afterlife, and carvings of family members with whom it was hoped they might be reunited. The poor, however, were buried in the ground, often close to such tombs.

Depending on the wealth of the family, the funeral procession may have included musicians and professional mourners. These were women who were employed to weep and wail with the women of the family, who may also have expressed their grief by pulling at their clothing and hair and throwing dust over their head and breasts, and several people may have been required to carry the dead person's possessions to the tomb. These would have been placed in the tomb with the coffin, as they were believed to be needed in the afterlife. Such funerary goods included food and drink, clothing, jewelry, and furniture, and in the case of kings, chariots and boats. At one time servants were even expected to kill themselves in order to be buried with their masters, but it became common practice instead to include models of servants and larger possessions, which were known as shabti or shawabti.

The Opening of the Mouth and Offerings

Once the coffin had been placed in its tomb, a last rite, known as the Opening of the Mouth ceremony, was performed by a priest or the dead person's son, which involved touching the mouth and other parts of the mummy, or in some cases a burial statue, with a stone tool, which was believed to restore the dead person's senses in the afterlife, and enable the ka spirit to receive sustenance. Burial statues in the tombs of the wealthiest people provided an alternative home for the spirit, whilst false doors marked the passageway between the worlds of the living and the dead. Elaborate tombs may also have had an adjoining chapel where prayers and food offerings could be made, but all families would have made such offerings regardless of wealth, in order to sustain the spirits in the afterlife. Once the ceremony had been completed, the tomb would be sealed and a feast held in honor of the dead.

Opposite above: Set of finger stalls, which preserved the fingers of the mummified royal body until they were restored in the afterlife.

Opposite below: This pair of funerary sandals, made from sheet gold, was found on the mummified body of the 22nd Dynasty king Sheshonq II. They were discovered in 1939 by French Egyptologist Pierre Montet at the Delta city of Tanis.

Right: Gold funerary mask of the 21st Dynasty king Psusennes I. His was one of a number of tombs unearthed in 1939 at Tanis, the necropolis for a number of rulers of the Third Intermediate Period.

Religion and the Gods

Although Egyptian religion was often surrounded by seemingly mysterious myths and ritual practices, it did in fact permeate all facets of life, not only shaping the political structure of the country, but nourishing and directing all aspects of Egyptian culture, from writing to art and monumental architecture. As in other cultures, a great deal of focus was placed on creation, the meaning of existence, and the possibility of an afterlife; from early nature-worship in tribal communities that venerated their leaders as a bridge to the divine, the pantheon of the gods, a code of moral standards and the divinity of kingship were established.

Early developments

Little is known of the religious beliefs and practices of Predynastic Egypt, but it is thought that the deities who were worshiped tended to be localized, gaining wider recognition and acceptance as smaller communities combined to form larger ones. In this way, the traits of various gods and goddesses began to be combined, and it became customary for the gods favored by ruling families to be elevated to greater status. At the beginning of the Old Kingdom, as important religious centers began to emerge, it seems that the priests at these cities made deliberate attempts to increase their power by cultivating specific theologies that made their chief gods central to the creation of the universe. The more important deities were grouped into families, enneads and ogdoads (the latter being groups typically comprised of nine and eight deities respectively). The most important of these groupings include the Ennead of Heliopolis, whose chief god was Atum; the Ogdoad of Hermopolis, where the chief god was Re; the Ptah-Sekhmet-Nefertem triad of Memphis, where the chief god was Ptah; the Khnum-Satet-Anuket triad of Elephantine, where the chief god was Khnum; and the Amun-Mut-Khonsu triad of Thebes, where the chief god was Amun.

The importance of kingship, whereby the king was seen as the mediator between the gods and the people, had already been established in earlier tribal communities, as had the association of animal forms with particular deities, and these characteristics were to continue throughout Dynastic Egypt as the theocratic system developed. Therefore, religion was already an established part of social and political life in early Egyptian history, with the king occupying a central role, and although beliefs

Below: Detail from a funerary text showing the sky goddess Nut spreading her wings over the deceased. As Nut was believed to swallow the sun each evening and give birth to it at dawn, she often featured in tomb imagery. It was a rift between Nut and Atum that was used by the Egyptians to account for the five extra days required to bring the 360-day Egyptian calendar in line with the solar year. Prevented from giving birth on any day of the Egyptian year, Nut was able to circumvent the ruling with the help of the moon god Thoth, who added five days to the calendar.

would undergo various transitions, and different cults would gain and lose favor at various points in Egypt's history, the fundamental elements that were in place at the foundation of the First Dynasty were to remain largely unchanged for thousands of years.

Atum at Heliopolis

The Ennead of Heliopolis, also known as the Great Ennead, is amongst the most important of the early groupings of deities, and its creation story was probably the most influential, with most of the later creation myths being simple variations on a theme. It consisted of Atum, sun-god and creator, who in the Heliopolitan creation myth sat on the primordial mound that emerged from the watery chaos of Nun, and created Shu (air) and Tefnut (moisture), who in turn produced Geb (the earth) and Nut (the sky), whose children were Osiris, Isis, Seth, and Nephthys. Essentially, the myth encapsulates the idea of maat, or the divine order of things, as Atum introduced order to chaos, allowing all things to come into being. Atum was sometimes represented in the form of a mythical bird, the Bennu, which was supposed to have alighted upon the mound of creation and the first place to be lit by the sun, the ben-ben. The first sun temples that emerged during the Old Kingdom housed a pyramid-shaped obelisk symbolizing the ben-ben, a shape that was immortalized in the great pyramids of Giza during the Third Dynasty.

Around the same time, the cult of the sun-god Re also rose to prominence at Hermopolis, and Atum was assimilated as Re-Atum, representing the setting sun, whilst Re would also be joined with Horus, represented by a falcon, to form Re-Harakhte, god of the horizon, or rising sun. It was believed that the sun-god traveled through the sky in a boat by day and through the Underworld at night, to be born anew each morning.

During the Old Kingdom, the cult of Re-Atum dominated, and the pharaohs took on the title "Son of Re," suggesting that the king was not only seen as a god, but as the progeny of the sun-god and creator himself.

Ptah at Memphis

The priesthood at Memphis attempted to rival that of Heliopolis, with a cosmogony, or creation myth, that established Ptah as having preceded Re-Atum. Ptah was identified as the primordial mound itself, who gave rise to creation through dreaming and speaking the names of everything that was then brought into being, including Atum, or Nefertum, the form of Atum as a youth. At the same time Sekhmet, who had been the war goddess of Upper Egypt, became Ptah's wife and the mother of Re-

Above: Sekhmet, goddess of war, was usually depicted with the head of a lioness.

Atum, completing the Ptah-Sekhmet-Nefertum triad. As the primordial mound and creator of all things, including lesser creator-gods, Ptah became the god of craftsmen, and was particularly associated with tombs, leading to his being considered a god of reincarnation.

The Cult of Osiris

By the end of the Old Kingdom, pharaonic power had been weakened, whilst that of the priesthood and nobility

Above: Wall painting from Nefertari's tomb depicting Osiris, king of the Underworld. His skin was sometimes white, representing the wrappings of the mummified corpse, and sometimes black, signifying the rich dark silt that underpinned Egypt's economy. Here it is green, symbol of regeneration.

Right: Statuette of the god Amun, from the temple dedicated to him at Karnak. Like the other Egyptian deities, Amun was associated with an animal: the ram, famed for its virility and belligerence. However, Amun was always depicted in human form.

had increased. This led to the start of a democratization of funerary beliefs, whereby the king was no longer seen as possessing the sole right of entry into the afterlife, and the nobility began to make their claims to immortality.

As unity was restored during the Middle Kingdom, so were many of the cult temples that had declined during the First Intermediate Period, and the importance of several gods was recognized, including Re-Atum at Heliopolis, Ptah at Memphis, and Amun at Thebes. However, it now seemed that the divinity of the king could no longer be relied upon to safeguard Egypt and its people, or provide them with safe passage into the afterlife, so the cult of

Osiris, the god with whom the king was said to be joined at death, became increasingly important and inclusive.

Osiris had originally been a fertility god, and a deification of the regrowth of crops, but as the myth of Osiris tells the story of his own death and resurrection, he also became associated with the Underworld and the afterlife. The cult center of Osiris was founded at Abydos, which was believed to be his burial place, and it became a site of mass pilgrimage and burial, as Egyptians believed that to associate themselves with Abydos would give them a better chance of enjoying eternal life. Thus, Abydos developed into one of the most important religious centers. Later, festivals celebrating the resurrection of Osiris would be held all over Egypt, and the belief developed that everyone would face a personal judgment upon death, offering Egyptians the possibility of immortality, regardless of their social standing.

The Hyksos

The Middle Kingdom came to an end with the invasion of the Asiatic Hyksos, or "Desert Princes," in the northern Delta region, which marked the start of the Second Intermediate Period, and the foundation of the 15th Dynasty. The Egyptian capital, Memphis, was sacked, and foreign deities were introduced, such as Astarte and Reshep, but the Hyksos generally adopted Egyptian habits

and customs, including the worship of gods such as Re, and Seth, god of the desert, storms, and chaos, who was approximately equivalent to their god Reshep, and religious life continued with little disruption.

Meanwhile, in the south of the country at Thebes, a line of Egyptian rulers, the kings of the 17th Dynasty, continued to control much of Upper Egypt, from Abydos to Elephantine, and as these kings' power increased, they would eventually overthrow the Hyksos to found the 18th Dynasty, heralding the beginning of the New Kingdom.

Amun at Thebes

As part of the Ogdoad of Hermopolis, Amun, "The Hidden One," had originally been a god of the air and winds, and one of the fundamental elements that had ultimately given rise to creation, but at Thebes, he came to be regarded as the creator in his own right, and was designated a wife, the divine mother Mut, and an adopted son, Menthu, the Theban god of war. However, over time, Menthu was replaced by Khonsu, an ancient moon-god, apparently on account of a crescent-shaped pool outside Mut's main temple, thus forming the Amun-Mut-Khonsu triad of Thebes.

Amun was sometimes represented as a goose, or associated with the ram, as a symbol of fertility, but he was most commonly depicted in human form, bearing a plumed crown, the feathers of which probably alluded to his former elemental status as an air deity.

Amun had been an important god at Thebes since the Old Kingdom, but following the expulsion of the Hyksos by the Thebans, his importance grew throughout the New Kingdom. At the beginning of that period, he was worshiped as a god of war, believed to have provided success in battle against the foreign invaders, but his increasing importance and influence soon led to him being seen as the creator father and king of all the gods, and Thebes as the very site of creation. Thebes in turn became the most important religious site in Egypt.

Throughout much of the 18th Dynasty, the priesthood of Amun at Thebes became increasingly powerful and wealthy, with control over what were now considered lesser deities, and eventually, Amun achieved the status of a national god, assimilating Re-Herakhty, the combined identities of Horus and Re, to form Amun-Re, the hidden aspect of the sun.

Right: Mut was a vulture goddess and was usually depicted in human form with a vulture headdress. When Amun rose to become king of the gods, Mut was installed as his divine consort. One of the meanings of "Mut" is "mother," indicative of her maternal aspect; she is often seen with outstretched wings to stress her protective role.

Above: Famed for her beauty, Nefertiti, principal wife of the 18th Dynasty king Akhenaten, wielded enormous power during Egypt's short-lived flirtation with monotheism in what is now known as the Amarna Period.

Opposite: This 13ft-high sandstone statue of Akhenaten adorned the Gempaaten temple site at Karnak. Akhenaten ordered temples dedicated to other gods to be closed, which would have impacted severely on Egypt's economy as well as revolutionizing the country's theological base.

Yet perhaps as a response to the increasing complexities of syncretism, that is, the merging of gods, and almost certainly as a response to the increasing power of the priesthood, Egypt was about to enter one of the most unusual and controversial periods in its history.

Akhenaten and Monotheism

During the reign of the 18th Dynasty's ninth king, Amenhotep III, increasing importance was attributed to another solar deity, the Aten, which had been known since the Middle Kingdom as the solar disk itself. However, in the early part of the 18th Dynasty, the Aten became more frequently referred to as a place where other solar deities such as Amun might reside and, in time came to be regarded as a god in its own right, the sun-god Aten, which assimilated Re-Herakhty, and was promoted above both the Heliopolitan creator Atum, and the Theban sun-god Amun-Re.

What was particularly unusual was that it was the royal court itself, rather than the priesthood, that elevated the Aten to the position of a deity in its own right. Furthermore, during the reign of Amenhotep III's son, Amenhotep IV, Aten would be promoted to the exclusion of all other deities, ushering in a period of monotheism, or the worship of one god, for the first time in Egyptian history.

In about year five or six of his reign, Amenhotep IV established a new capital north of Thebes, Akhetaten, meaning "Horizon of the Aten," now known as el-Amarna, where a great temple to Aten was constructed. Around this time, the king also changed his name to Akhenaten, or "Servant of the Aten," and began to actively suppress the worship of all other gods, ordering the closure of temples and, in particular, defacing the name and image of Amun wherever it occurred.

Worship of earlier manifestations of the sun, including Re, Herakhty, Khepri, Atum, and Amun, was outlawed, and Aten was transformed from the solar disk into the sole god and creator that gave life through its illuminating rays. Additionally, Akhenaten elevated his own divine status, and by association that of his family, by proclaiming that Aten had been revealed only to himself, and that he was the sole interpreter of Aten's commandments.

In the process, the Aten was distanced from both the general populace and the priesthood, which would have undermined any attempt to elevate Aten as the sole god amongst the people. For whilst the king's court undoubtedly embraced the new official religion, with no direct relationship to the god, no accompanying mythology, and no cult statue, it is unlikely that ordinary Egyptians did. Instead they probably continued to worship traditional deities in their homes as they always had, despite the fact that only images of the royal family were now permitted in homes and temples alike.

The Art of the Amarna Period

Akhenaten's dramatic break from conventional Egyptian religion coincided with the introduction of a new artistic style in official art that was characterized by increased realism, and flowing, rather than rigid, lines particularly with regard to the human form. The content of official art from this period generally also became less formal than had been seen in earlier dynastic times, with Akhenaten and his family depicted engaging in more personal and intimate activities. However, their worship of the Aten itself, as a disk whose rays took the form of outstretched hands, also featured significantly.

Most unusually, Akhenaten, his family, and sometimes other members of the royal court were often represented with a very strange physique, with elongated heads, necks and limbs, a distended belly and swollen breasts, thighs, and buttocks. Some theorists have suggested that this may have been the result of illness, whilst others put forward the idea that it may be simply an artistic exaggeration.

Akhenaten's wife, Nefertiti, also features very prominently in Amarna artworks, and is often depicted wearing a crown, either alongside her husband, or in ways normally reserved for the pharaohs themselves, such as engaged in battle or smiting captives with a mace. This suggests that she may have played a particularly important role in the royal household, and may have held a great deal of influence over Akhenaten.

The Restoration of Amun

The religious upheaval brought about by Akhenaten's rule was highly unpopular, especially amongst the previous priesthoods whose power had been taken away, and soon after his death, polytheism, or the worship of several gods, was reinstated and traditional forms of worship, including the celebration of cult festivals, were resumed. Following the brief reign of Smenkhkare, which was probably actually a coregency with Akhenaten, the young Tutankhaten, who is thought to have been Akhenaten's son, was crowned pharaoh at Thebes, and changed his name to Tutankhamun, or "the living image of Amun," thereby reinstating power at Thebes and restoring Amun as the most important of the gods.

Akhenaten was now considered a heretic and the city of Akhenaten was demolished, monuments were destroyed, and over time the names and images of the Amarna kings were largely eradicated from history, including being omitted from the king-lists. Aten was similarly removed from the pantheon of Egyptian deities, and until Christianity became established during the Roman rule of Egypt, Amun would remain the most pre-eminent of the gods.

Anubis

Anubis was the jackal-headed god of the dead and embalming. Jackals were common scavengers around cemeteries, and Egyptians revered them by way of appeasement, fearing the desecration of graves. Before Osiris became king of the Underworld, Anubis was Judge of the Dead. Thereafter Anubis was accommodated in the judgment proceedings as the bastard son of Osiris and Nephthys. He supervised the Weighing of the Heart ceremony, which took place before Osiris, and was the custodian of the dead on their journey to the afterlife. Anubis' flesh was black, a color associated with regeneration as the dark silt deposits left by the annual inundation breathed new life into the soil. Anubis' skin was thus a symbol of rebirth rather than decay.

At first Anubis was exclusively concerned with the burial rites of pharaohs, but became a god of the dead for all Egyptians as funereal rituals under-

Below: In a vignette from the Book of the Dead, the deceased kneels before Anubis, god of mummification. The Book of the Dead consisted of some 200 spells, many derived from the earlier Pyramid and Coffin Texts. Unlike the earlier funerary texts, which were the exclusive preserve of royalty and the wealthy, the Book of the Dead was available to anyone who could afford a papyrus copy. The Book of the Dead was placed either inside the coffin or within the wrappings of the mummified body.

went a democratization process. Priests carrying out embalming procedures wore jackal-headed masks to resemble Anubis.

Isis

A goddess of obscure origin, Isis became the divine mother of the reigning king by virtue of her place in the Heliopolitan Ennead. Isis was the daughter of Geb and Nut and sister-wife of King Osiris. Her valiant efforts in trying to restore her murdered husband to life, together with the lengths she went to in protecting her son, Horus, made Isis the archetypal loyal wife and devoted mother. She was sometimes depicted with wings, a reference to the fact that she changed herself into a kite and hovered over Osiris in an effort to breathe new life into him. During the New Kingdom Isis was often represented as a cow goddess, an animal associated with fecundity and a nurturing role.

Above: The "wedjat" or "healed eye" featured prominently in Egyptian funeral iconography.

Right: Sculpture depicting Isis suckling the infant Horus.

Many reliefs and statuettes show Isis suckling the infant Horus. Isis merged with several other gods during the Late Period. Her cult spread beyond Egypt's shores, and to many parts of the Roman Empire during Rome's period of dominion. Temples to Isis were erected in Rome itself, and her popularity rivaled that of the traditional Roman pantheon. She was revered and worshiped long after Egypt had converted to Christianity.

Horus

The falcon god Horus was associated with kingship from the beginning of the Dynastic Period. He was not the only deity represented in the form of a hawk, but over time the others were either displaced or assimilated within the persona of Horus, around whom many myths grew. As the son of Isis, Horus engaged in a long struggle to defeat the evil Seth, murderer of his father Osiris. At first Re chose the experience of Seth over Horus's immaturity, and the latter is sometimes depicted as a child with the sidelock of youth. One account of the nephew–uncle battle describes a harpoon fight, in which both Horus and Seth are wounded. Isis helps her son, but also assists her evil brother Seth when he is struck. Enraged, Horus chops off his mother's head and disappears into the mountains. Isis, magically healed by Re, forgives her son. Seth pursues Horus and gouges out his eyes, but his sight is restored by Hathor. The "wedjat" or "healed eye" became one of the powerful symbols of protection, often painted on coffins or used in amulet form. After a heated exchange of letters between Re and Osiris, now king of the Underworld, Horus was granted the throne. The reigning Egyptian king was regarded as the living Horus, while deceased rulers were associated with Osiris. The mythology of the Ennead was used as a means of legitimizing succession to the throne. Whoever presided over the burial of the previous ruler was believed to be acting as Horus, irrespective of whether there was a blood tie between himself and the dead king.

Temples

The Ancient Egyptians worshiped hundreds of different gods and goddesses. Some were connected to the forces of nature, such as the weather, the Nile, the sun, and the moon, and many others were related to aspects of everyday life, such as the home, but as the pharaoh was also worshiped as a god on Earth, two main types of temple were constructed: cult temples, which were dedicated to one or more deities, and royal, or mortuary temples, which were built in honor of the pharaoh.

Cult Temples

Cult temples were known to the Egyptians as "hat-netcher," meaning "god's house," as they believed that the ka spirits of their gods and goddesses actually dwelt in the temple, within a statue in the temple's inner sanctum, or naos.

Cult temples were often large complexes, containing stores, granaries, schools, and workshops, but regardless of their size, they all shared a basic layout. A main gateway or pylon would lead to an open courtyard, beyond which was the roofed hypostyle hall, which contained many columns. These were often carved and decorated to resemble papyrus reeds, crowned with lotus blossom motifs, which symbolized creation and the unfolding of the

universe, and the hall sloped upward toward the inner sanctum, representing the first mound of earth to have arisen from the waters of chaos at the beginning of time.

Theoretically, only the pharaoh was deemed holy enough to enter the inner sanctum, but in practice, the highest-ranking priests were entitled to enter in order to carry out the necessary daily rituals, which included waking the deity each day with a hymn, burning incense, washing, anointing and clothing the statue, and presenting it with offerings of food. These priests also had to wash themselves four times a day and would shave all the hair from their heads and bodies as a form of ritual purification. The most important priests may have lived and worked at

Above: Aerial view of the Temple of Amun, with the Temple of Montu and the modern village of Karnak to the right.

Left: From the Early Dynastic era the ram was a potent symbol, with its obvious connection with fertility. Several gods were depicted in the form of a ram, the most important of whom was Khnum. This line of ram-headed sphinxes stands guard over the Temple of Amun at Karnak.

Opposite: The Temple of Luxor, dedicated to Amun, was begun during the Middle Kingdom but it was Amenhotep III who was chiefly responsible for creating the complex as it is today. Its main purpose was as a setting for the annual opet festival, when a cult statue of Amun was borne from Karnak to Luxor. This ceremonial procession was associated with fertility, of both Amun and, by extension, the reigning pharaoh.

Karnak

Cult temples were the most important buildings in Egyptian towns and cities, and some accumulated vast amounts of wealth, particularly during the New Kingdom. The temple complex at Karnak became the largest in Egypt, consisting of a main temple dedicated to Amun and smaller temples for his wife Mut and son Khonsu. It was begun during the Middle Kingdom and continued to be expanded throughout the New Kingdom by a succession of kings, with the addition of huge gateways and obelisks. Ramesses II contributed huge statues of himself, and oversaw the completion of the Great Hypostyle Hall, which contained 134 carved columns, some of which were over 66 feet tall.

the temple throughout the year, but others would spend time engaged in matters outside of the temple, such as collecting taxes and other administrative duties. Originally there were also priestesses, but by the time of the New Kingdom, only men were permitted to be priests. However, female musicians continued to perform during temple ceremonies.

Ordinary people were not permitted to enter beyond the first courtyard, and would generally worship their gods at home at small shrines, but they would come to the temple to leave offerings and say prayers, and at certain times of the year would celebrate festival days, when the cult statues would be carried on ceremonial journeys in wooden shrines that often resembled boats.

Mortuary Temples

Although mortuary temples were dedicated to the memory of dead pharaohs, as places where they could be honored once they had died, it was also believed that their construction was necessary for the king to gain entry to the afterlife, and so building work usually began almost as soon as a new pharaoh came to the throne. Additionally, ceremonies were sometimes held in them while the king was still alive, such as rituals to reinforce the pharaoh's divinity. Once a pharaoh had died, however, it was believed that he became one with the gods, and, like them, required a house on Earth to which his ka spirit could return in order to receive sustenance, in the form of offerings of food. In the same way that statues of gods and goddesses were enshrined in the cult temples, a statue of the pharaoh would be placed in his mortuary temple, where these offerings could be made.

Throughout the main period of pyramid building during the Old Kingdom, mortuary temples were constructed as part of the pyramid complex, and were positioned to face the rising sun on the east side of a pyramid, but during the New Kingdom, when the pharaohs were buried in the more remote Valley of the Kings, their mortuary temples were often built some distance away from their tombs. Few mortuary temples have survived intact, as although the continuity of the royal and divine lineage was considered important, many pharaohs reused the stone from a predecessor's temple in order to construct their own.

Above: The gateway to the Temple of Luxor, flanked by seated statues of Ramesses II. It lies just over one mile south of the vast temple complex at Karnak, the two sites linked by an avenue of sphinxes.

Agriculture and Food

Although Egypt is an arid country, surrounded by hot, dry desert, which is unsuitable for growing crops, the civilization of Ancient Egypt was essentially founded on agriculture, with the main settlements being established on the narrow strips of land alongside the River Nile where the soil was most fertile, and where crops such as wheat, barley, fruit, and vegetables could be grown successfully. Additionally, the Ancient Egyptians kept a variety of animals for food, skins, and wool, as well as for working the land. They also fished in the Nile and hunted for birds and other animals along the banks of the river and in the surrounding deserts.

The Farming Year

With so little rainfall, agriculture in Egypt was entirely dependent upon the waters of the River Nile, and the farming calendar was divided into three seasons, which revolved around the Nile's changing water levels. These seasons were that of flooding, which was also known as Akhet, or "the Inundation"; plowing and planting, known as Peret, or "coming forth," and finally, harvest time, or Shemu, "the time of drought."

The annual flood typically began in Egypt around June or July, when the Nile was swollen by melting snow and spring rains far to the south in the Ethiopian mountains, and lasted until about September, when the waters would recede, having deposited a highly fertile silt along the river banks, which could then be prepared for farming. This rich black mud was essential for the growth of crops, and also provided the Egyptians with their word for their country, "Kemet," or "the Black Land." The storage and regulation of water throughout the rest of the year was also of the utmost importance, and the Ancient Egyptians developed a network of dams, dykes, canals, and irrigation channels with which to store the floodwater, and control its flow to the fields. Shadufs, or counterweighted buckets, which were mounted on beams, were then used to transfer water from these channels.

Following the recession of the floodwater, the season of plowing and planting would begin around October. Firstly the land would be divided into fields by low mud walls. The soil would be hoed and tilled, and the seed sown by hand, before being pushed into the ground by oxen-drawn plows. Often, cattle or sheep would subsequently be driven over the earth to insure that the seed was well trodden in.

The harvest began in March or April once the crops had grown, and consisted of three stages: firstly the crops would be cut with sickles and the ears of grain gathered, before being taken to the threshing floor, where they would be trampled by donkeys or cattle, or flailed, in order to separate the grain from the husks, or chaff. Finally, this was winnowed, or scooped into the air, so that the chaff would be carried away by the wind, leaving the heavier grain behind. Once the harvest was complete, taxes in the form of a percentage of the crop would be collected, as all the land was effectively owned by the pharaoh, or king.

Right: Wall painting from the tomb of Menna showing the harvesting of wheat which would be gathered and transported to be threshed in large baskets, either mounted on donkeys or carried on long poles.

Baking and Brewing

As barley and wheat were the main cereal crops produced by the Ancient Egyptians, the staple diet for most people would have consisted of bread and beer, and as these were consumed with most meals, a great deal of time would have been spent both baking and brewing. This would have been an everyday activity for ordinary women, whilst wealthy Egyptians would have bought their bread from bakers, or employed servants to provide their food, and would also have enjoyed a much more varied diet.

Bread was made by grinding grain between stones to produce flour, to which water and other ingredients such as honey or herbs may have been added, and the dough would then have been shaped in molds before being baked in, or on the outside of, a clay oven, or in pots over a fire.

Beer was made by crumbling bread into a vat of water that had been sweetened with honey, or fruit such as dates, and left to ferment before being strained into jars and sealed.

Fruit, Vegetables, Meat, and Fish

In addition to barley and wheat, the Ancient Egyptians grew flax with which to make linen for clothes, vegetables such as beans, lentils, onions, leeks, cucumbers, and lettuces, and a variety of fruits, including grapes, dates, figs, and pomegranates, from which wine could be made. They also made cheese, drank milk, and ate eggs, and various livestock was raised, including antelope, cattle, sheep, goats, pigs, ducks, and geese. Wildfowl would also have been hunted for meat, as were animals such as hyenas. However, although food was generally not in short supply, only the wealthy could regularly afford to eat meat and drink wine. Beef was highly prized, whilst pork and fish were often seen as unclean. Nevertheless, fish were plentiful in the Nile, and would have supplemented the diet of ordinary people.

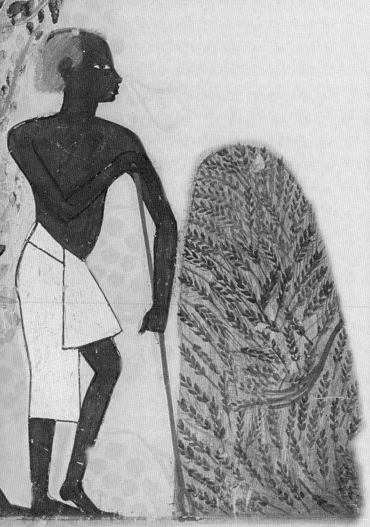

Top: Model of a servant (shabti) carrying loaves and meat. Whilst bread was a staple, meat was eaten regularly only by the wealthy.

Above: Painting from the tomb of Nakt depicting men gathering grapes from an arbor. The grapes were trampled by foot and the liquid left to ferment in tall jars.

Cooking and Dining

Due to the heat, smoke and smells, most cooking would have taken place outside at the rear of the house, either in a clay oven, or on a tripod or spit over a fire, but the poorest people would have cooked indoors, over a fire pit in the floor of their homes. Everyone would have eaten with their fingers, with adults seated on simple stools at low tables, whilst children would have sat on the floor.

Banquets

Ordinary Egyptians may have celebrated special occasions such as marriages and births with feasts or banquets, but banquets were more commonly the preserve of the rich, who would have entertained guests with lavish meals prepared by servants. Meat, vegetables, fruit, cakes and wine would have been served to guests, who would attend in their best clothes, jewelry and make-up. Wax incense cones were also worn on the top of the heads, and guests were sometimes entertained by musicians and dancers.

Right: Agricultural scenes were often depicted in tombs as it was believed that, after death, one would enter an idealized "Field of Reeds." This detail from a wall painting in the tomb of Sennedjem shows a farmer and his wife at work in the "Field of Reeds."

Families and Children

The Ancient Egyptians placed a great deal of emphasis on family life, and children, who made up a large part of the population, were held in high regard. Similarly, the elderly were also well respected, and despite a high infant mortality rate and an average life expectancy of perhaps thirty-five to forty years, families often had as many as five children and lived in extended groups, as it was common for a married couple to live with the husband's parents until he had acquired enough wealth to buy or construct a home for himself, his wife and children.

Adulthood began at the onset of puberty, at which time "the sidelock of youth" would be removed, and marriage occurred remarkably young by today's standards: when girls were perhaps twelve years old and boys around fifteen. There was no formal wedding ceremony; rather, a contract would be drawn up, listing the property and possessions that both the man and woman would bring to the marriage, and hence it was common for cousins to marry in order to keep property within a family. A woman was free to choose her husband, but she would often be introduced to a potential partner by her parents.

Men were theoretically allowed more than one wife, although this was uncommon outside the ruling families, and although a woman's infidelity could be punished by death, men and women were otherwise essentially regarded as equals. Women could own and inherit property, undertake business transactions, appear as witnesses in court and hold jobs outside the family home. However, it was usual for a woman to run the household, prepare food, and care for her children, perhaps whilst also working from home, weaving or baking for example. Girls would learn housekeeping skills from their mothers, whilst boys would begin to follow in their fathers' footsteps from an early age, either working in agriculture or learning a trade.

During the Old Kingdom, few children were formally educated other than the sons of scribes, who would have been taught at home by their fathers from the age of about nine. In later times, however, these children, and those of other important or wealthy people, were educated together at schools.

Pregnancy and birth

Although pregnancy was welcomed, it was highly dangerous for both mother and child, and perhaps as a result was surrounded by ritual and myth. Nevertheless, there is also some evidence to suggest that the Egyptians were good at gauging fertility, detecting pregnancy at an early stage, making a diagnosis of twins, and predicting the gender of unborn children.

There were many gods and goddesses associated with fertility, pregnancy, and birth, including Khnum, the creator, Isis and Hathor, who were mother-goddesses, Bes, the protector of children, and Tawaret, goddess of childbirth, who was most commonly represented as a pregnant hippopotamus.

During delivery, incantations were chanted and wands carved with depictions of protective gods and goddesses were used, whilst, more practically, crushed poppy seeds soaked in beer were administered for pain relief, and birthing took place squatting or kneeling on special brick platforms or wooden stools.

Ordinary women would give birth in the presence of friends and family, carry their offspring in a sling wrapped around the body, and breastfeed until their child was about three years old. The wealthy, however, could afford to employ specialist midwives, servants, and wet-nurses to help deliver and care for their newborn children.

Left: Akhenaten kisses one of his daughters in a typically intimate family scene from the Amarna Period. Nefertiti bore Akhenaten six daughters, two of whom the king married in an attempt to produce a male heir.

Opposite: Detail of a stela from el-Amarna showing Nefertiti with two of her daughters on her lap while a third receives a gift from Akhenaten. Cranial distortion was typical in the art of the Amarna Period.

Sport and Recreation

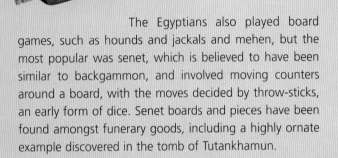

Many ordinary Egyptians undertook hard physical labor and were no doubt very fit, whereas for the wealthy, corpulence, or being well fed, was seen as a symbol of status. Regardless of social standing, however, all members of society are known to have enjoyed some form of recreational activity, from playing board games to hunting, and enjoying religious festivities and other celebrations, either as spectators or performers.

Hunting and fishing were necessary in order to provide food, but various animals were also pursued for sport. People hunted with dogs in the desert for hares, antelope, ostriches, foxes, hyenas, and lions, and used cats to flush wildfowl along the marshy banks of the Nile, which were then brought down with throwing sticks. Hippos and crocodiles were also hunted for sport, and the pharaohs themselves would take part in hunting for these most dangerous animals, as well as lions, in order to prove their prowess. People also swam in the Nile, and held boating competitions, where they would try to dislodge each other from their vessels with wooden poles.

Although physical fitness was not always regarded as a positive attribute, in times of war it would certainly have been seen as such, and many aspects of military training, including running, boxing, wrestling, fencing, archery, boat-handling, and chariot-racing also became civilian pursuits. Gymnastics was popular too, as were long jump, high jump, and weightlifting by the 25th Dynasty.

At banquets and times of religious festival, people were entertained by professional acrobats, magicians, jugglers, dancers, and musicians, and instruments included wooden and reed flutes, harps, lutes, zithers, lyres, drums, tambourines, bells, rattles, and castanets. Little is known of Egyptian music and dancing, although it is thought to have originally been rather slow and stately until the later influence of Asian cultures. There were also poets and storytellers, but no real theater other than the dramatization of the lives of the gods, which were performed at temples and in royal processions during times of festivity.

Children played games such as leap-frog, piggyback and blind-man's-buff, and had wooden animal toys, some with moving parts, balls made of clay, leather, or papyrus, and dolls, although the latter may also have served as symbolic or ritual objects.

The Egyptians also played board games, such as hounds and jackals and mehen, but the most popular was senet, which is believed to have been similar to backgammon, and involved moving counters around a board, with the moves decided by throw-sticks, an early form of dice. Senet boards and pieces have been found amongst funerary goods, including a highly ornate example discovered in the tomb of Tutankhamun.

Above: Gaming board and pieces to play either senet or "twenty squares." The former was a very popular game, in which two players vied to move their pieces round the board. Certain squares represented good or ill fortune, leading to speculation that when included in funerary equipment, senet assumed symbolic significance.

Below: Sketch of an acrobatic dancer painted on a shard of limestone. Professional acrobats often entertained at banquets and religious festivals.

Opposite: Banqueting scene from the tomb-chapel of Nebamun. Musicians provide the music, one playing the double flute while another claps out a rhythmic accompaniment.

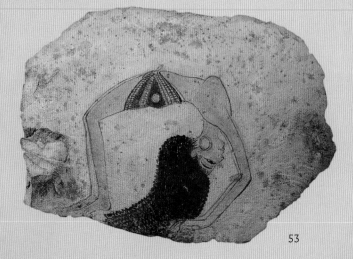

Crafts and Technology

Although the tools and techniques employed by the Ancient Egyptians were relatively simple, the artifacts that were produced were typically of very high quality, and as a result, craftsmen of various kinds were well respected and usually well paid members of society, whose skills were in great demand.

There were, however, differing levels of expertise and workmanship, varying from those producing simple everyday items such as pottery and woven baskets for the home, to luxury items for the wealthy. The most skillful artisans were employed by officials and even the pharaoh himself, and worked on the most ornate artifacts and wall paintings for the royal tombs, temples, and palaces.

Craftsmen included potters, jewelers, masons, carpenters, and glass, textile, and metalworkers. Originally a worker would have undertaken the entire production of an artifact by himself, although, by the end of the Old Kingdom, an early form of mass production had been established. Craftsmen began to work

together in workshops overseen by foremen and scribes, and workers began to specialize in particular fields of production, such as glazing or painting, leading to a higher standard of workmanship and better quality products.

However, despite a certain level of innovation and development, the Ancient Egyptians were seldom at the forefront of technological advance. They often seem to have been somewhat reluctant to adopt new or outside technologies and techniques, perhaps largely as a result of their religious beliefs and social ideals and structure.

Carpentry

Wood was in fairly short supply in Egypt, but nevertheless the Egyptians were excellent carpenters, and with the development of copper

Above: Wooden model of carpenters at work, found in the tomb of Meketre at Deir el-Bahri.

Left: Relief fragment from a 19th Dynasty tomb showing a carpenter at work using an adze. Everyday scenes of work and leisure were used to create a perfect mortal world, which would be recreated in the eternal life. The disheveled appearance of this worker is something of an aberration in tomb imagery.

tools during the Early Dynastic Period came greatly improved woodwork, and the application of techniques such as mortice-and-tenon joints, dovetailing and mitring. Tools included saws, axes, chisels, mallets, adzes, punches, and bow-drills; local woods such as sycamore, fig, and palm would have been used for simple items of furniture, whilst imported woods like ebony and cedar would have been used in the construction of more elaborate pieces for the wealthy.

Stone, Ceramics, and Glass

Masons worked with several materials including limestone, sandstone, granite, alabaster, basalt, quartzite, and slate to produce everything from huge statues to stone tools, cosmetic palettes, and vessels. Originally jars would have been laboriously carved from stone, but following the development of the potter's wheel and the chimney kiln around the 5th Dynasty, most jars, bowls and other containers would have been made of clay pottery. These were sometimes decoratively painted, and later the application of glazes was introduced. An important material in the production of glazed items was faience, a blue glass-like substance that was made by heating crushed quartz, used for vessels, tiles, beads, inlaid work, and jewelry. It was a common alternative to precious or semiprecious stones such as turquoise and lapis lazuli.

Glass was later adopted for the same purpose, and also to produce small vessels. This was initially achieved by applying molten glass to a mold, before glass-blowing was adopted during the Ptolemaic Period.

Metalwork

Gold had been mined since Predynastic times, and was used for jewelry, inlaying furniture and applied as gold leaf to all manner of objects, including statues, furniture, coffins, and even walls, but copper smelting, which was well developed by the Early Dynastic Period, enabled the production of tools, weapons, cooking utensils, and items such as pins, tweezers, razors, and burnished mirrors. Other metals used included silver and electrum, a mixture of gold and silver, and later, primarily during the New Kingdom, bronze came into widespread use, although it had been known to the Egyptians some 500 years earlier. Metals were melted in pottery crucibles over charcoal-burning furnaces, which, until the introduction of foot-worked bellows, were blown with reed pipes. The molten metal was then poured into molds, cooled, and hammered into shape.

Jewelry

Almost everyone in Ancient Egypt would have worn some jewelry regardless of their social status, although the amount worn and the quality of workmanship would have varied accordingly. In addition to being decorative, amulets or charms were also worn in the belief that they would provide protection from illness and bring good luck. Jewelers worked with gold, silver, electrum, hematite, and a number of semiprecious and precious stones, including lapis lazuli, turquoise, jasper, feldspar, amethyst, garnet, and cornelian, in order to produce rings, earrings, bangles, necklaces, and diadems. Jewelry, particularly amulets, also featured prominently amongst funerary goods, and in fact

Above: Glass unguent or cosmetics jar, dating from the Amarna Period of the 18th Dynasty. Glass-making did not appear in Egypt until the Middle Kingdom.

Below: Middle Kingdom statuette of a hippopotamus, made from blue faience and decorated with images of papyrus and other water plants. The male hippopotamus, along with the crocodile, was deemed a threat to both people and crops and thus a force for evil.

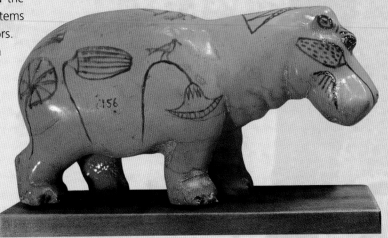

was placed at specific points on the body when mummies were wrapped, although in many cases, such jewelry would have been made of faience, plaster, and wood.

Textiles

Due to the hot climate, few clothes were worn, and in fact servants are often depicted naked, but most people would have worn simple garments: short kilts or loincloths for men and long dresses for women. Animal skins were sometimes worn, and armor is known to have been made from leather and crocodile skin, but most clothing was made from linen, which was light and airy. Linen was obtained from the stems of the flax plant, which would be harvested and then soaked in water for several days in order to separate and soften the fibers. Following this, the stems would be beaten to further soften them, and then the fibers would be attached to a spindle to be twisted into threads. Finally, these threads would be woven on a simple loom to form linen cloth. Spinning and weaving were performed both at home and in workshops, and were undertaken almost exclusively by women until the time of the New Kingdom, when men began to work on large upright looms, making patterned cloths. The best linen produced was incredibly fine, and would have been almost transparent.

Opposite: Glass fragment of a theatrical mask of the Greco-Roman Period, showing a hetaira, or courtesan.

Left: Cosmetic spoon in the form of a young woman carrying an amphora on her shoulder. Items of cosmetic equipment and the jars into which the cosmetics were decanted were often highly embellished.

Writing

Hieroglyphics

The earliest form of Egyptian writing is thought to have been developed as a result of Sumerian influence around 3200 BC, prior to the start of the Dynastic Period, and was last used in about AD 395, on the walls of the Isis Temple on the island of Philae. However, its use was already in decline by the fourth century AD, due to the fact that Egypt had undergone a Christian conversion and adopted the Greek alphabet and Coptic script.

The Egyptians called their language "mdw ntr" or "medu-netjer," meaning "words of the gods," but the Greeks gave it the name "hieroglyphics." This translates as "sacred inscriptions" or "sacred carvings," reflecting both the fact that the Egyptians believed the written word to be a gift from the gods, and that it was commonly carved in stone, initially on slates, and later, more grandly, into the walls of tombs and temples. For the Egyptians, writing, art, and religion were seen as interconnected, and the hieroglyphic language was originally used by the priesthood in religious and official texts, and to illuminate religious paintings. However hieroglyphs could also be seen as decorative in their own right, and in addition to being used for monumental inscriptions, they were applied to furniture, coffins, sarcophagi, and scrolls, often in great detail and in several colors.

Hieroglyphic writing is pictorial, that is, distinguishable pictures or symbols are used to express objects and ideas, but single symbols and groups of symbols would also come to represent the sounds of the spoken language, with the simplest hieroglyphs that represented the alphabetic sounds being combined to make more complex sounds or entire words. An extra symbol, known as a "determinative," would often be placed at the end of a word to clarify its meaning; for example, a symbol of either a man or a woman would be used to indicate the gender of the subject or speaker in a sentence. Some symbols were also employed in the belief that they had magical, often protective, properties.

By the Middle Kingdom, more than 750 hieroglyphs were in use, and in fact throughout its long history, hieroglyphic writing underwent various changes in its style, composition, and application. The first instance of hieroglyphic writing, which is sometimes known as "Old Egyptian," may be considered the language of the Old Kingdom, but by the First Intermediate Period this had evolved into "Middle Egyptian," continued until the Greco-Roman Period. In addition to its use in monumental and religious texts, this also appeared in literature and medical and scientific texts until the Second Intermediate Period. By the 18th Dynasty, at the beginning of the New Kingdom, a new vernacular, "Late Egyptian" had evolved, mainly for letters and business documents, but it was also used for literary texts and monumental inscriptions from the 19th Dynasty onward.

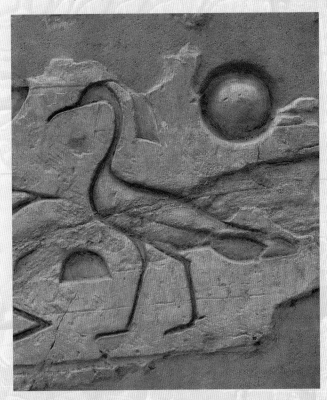

Opposite: Hieroglyphs and the cartouche of Ramesses II at the Temple of Luxor.

Right: Hieroglyph representing the crested ibis, which was used to express the word akh. Egyptians believed that a person's ba and ka—roughly equating to personality and spirit —had to be reunited after death before a person could successfully take his place in the Underworld.

Hieratic

Hieratic writing is almost as old as hieroglyphics, having appeared during the 2nd Dynasty, around 2700 BC, and it is based on hieroglyphic forms. However, it is a cursive script, or handwriting, that was developed through writing on papyrus or linen with a reed brush. Pictorial details that clearly defined one symbol from another, in terms of both appearance and meaning, were often omitted as the symbols became more letter-like in shape, and easier and faster to write, but for the most important hieratic texts careful calligraphy would have been used. "Hieratic" comes from the Greek word meaning "priestly," as by the time of the Greek arrival in Egypt, this script was used almost entirely for religious texts, but before the development of demotic script, it was also used for more mundane tasks, such as administrative writings.

Demotic

Demotic script emerged during the Late Dynastic Period, around the time of the 25th or 26th Dynasty, as a further development of hieratic, and was written with an even faster hand. In this way, new symbols or characters were formed that marked a greater shift away from hieroglyphics. "Demotic" comes from the Greek word "demotikos" meaning "popular," as although writing was only performed by scribes and the majority of the population was illiterate, demotic script was used for all manner of purposes, including business, legal, and literary texts, as well as occasionally in inscriptions.

Coptic

The last form of the Ancient Egyptian language is known as Coptic, which was developed as a means of translating Christian religious texts into an accessible form for the Egyptians. By this time, Greek culture predominated, and so Coptic script utilized the letters of the Greek alphabet, with the addition of seven symbols drawn from hieroglyphics. These were used to represent Egyptian letter sounds that were absent from Greek. Following the Arab conquest of Egypt in AD 640, and the subsequent conversion of most Egyptians to Islam, Arabic became the main language of Egypt, but Coptic would continue to be used by the Christian minority in Egypt for several more centuries.

The Rosetta Stone

During the period of Greek rule in Egypt, the Ancient Egyptian languages died out and so an understanding of them became lost, but it also seems that the Greeks never really understood hieroglyphics as a language, but thought of it as a code, which was designed to hide esoteric knowledge. For over 1000 years, nobody could decipher the meaning of hieroglyphics, but this changed after the discovery of the Rosetta Stone in AD 1799. This tablet of black basalt bore three

Left: Scribes were part of the elite in Ancient Egyptian society. They were not simply clerical workers but senior officials involved in all aspects of government. In artwork scribes were invariably portrayed sitting cross-legged with a papyrus scroll on their knees.

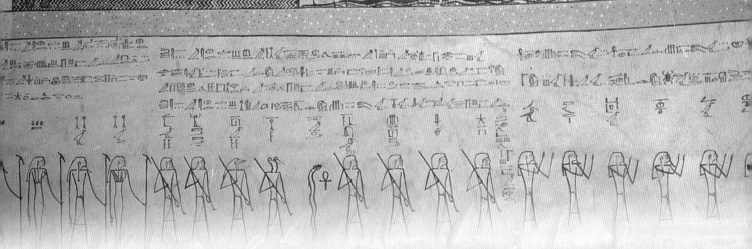

inscriptions: one in hieroglyphics, one in demotic, and the last in Greek, and by comparing these inscriptions with other texts, including those found on part of an obelisk that was also written in hieroglyphics and Greek, it was eventually realized that they bore the same message, and that hieroglyphics was a decipherable script. This work was begun by a British doctor, Thomas Young, around 1819 and taken up by a young French scholar, Jean-François Champollion, who by 1822 had been able to translate the names of more than seventy of the kings of Egypt, and would go on to translate several more texts. The mystery of hieroglyphs had finally been solved, and by studying them, scholars have been able to learn most of what we know today about life in Ancient Egypt.

Papyrus

Papyrus is a plant that was once common in the Nile Delta and Valley, and was used by the Egyptians for several purposes, including matting, boat-building, and basket, rope, and sandal-making, but one of the most common uses was in making papyrus sheets for writing on, and it is actually from papyrus that we get the word "paper."

To form papyrus sheets, the coarse outer part of the stem was removed, then the softer, pithy core was cut into narrow strips, which were laid next to each other. A second layer of strips would be laid across these, horizontally, and the papyrus was then pressed or beaten with a mallet to bond them together. Once dry, a tough sheet of papyrus was produced, which could be joined to others to form long scrolls. The longest of these that has been discovered is the Great Harris Papyrus, which is over 135 feet long, and is now housed in the British Museum. Like many Egyptian artifacts, papyrus was often well preserved by the arid climate of Egypt, and the oldest are thought to date from long before the Early Dynastic Period, but papyrus continued to be used well after the time of the pharaohs, until it was gradually replaced by cloth paper from the Far East.

Papyrus was originally used for religious texts, and because it flourished as a result of the life-giving Nile, it had a symbolic importance of its own, being associated with creation. For this reason, papyrus designs often featured in temple architecture and the papyrus plant became the royal symbol of Lower Egypt.

Above: Painted scene from the wall of Tuthmosis III's tomb in the Valley of the Kings. The images are from the Amduat, the book of "that which is in the netherworld." This covered a number of funerary texts describing the Sun God's journey through the night sky and rebirth at the new dawn. It also contained spells which protected the deceased king on his journey to the afterlife.

Below: King-list from the temple of Ramesses II at Abydos. It records Ramesses' offerings to his predecessors, whose names are recorded in rows of cartouches. All incumbent kings did this as a means of establishing their own legitimacy in the royal line.

Clothing and Jewelry

Unlike the members of some civilizations, the Ancient Egyptians were not ashamed of nudity, and it was customary for children and servants to be naked. Many people may also have gone unclothed during the hot summer months, and whilst several items of clothing have been discovered, it is known that the Egyptians generally wore very little, and those items that were worn were simple linen garments such as wrap-around kilts, skirts, and dresses, although fitted shirts and dresses were also worn.

Linen was produced from flax plants that grew along the banks of the Nile, and was used to manufacture the clothes worn by everyone, regardless of their social status. However, the clothing worn by the poor would have been much more coarsely woven than the fine linen worn by the wealthy, whose garments were also embellished with feathers and beads to add color and decoration.

Colored dyes such as henna and saffron began to be used during the Old Kingdom, and the weaving of colored patterns was introduced with the vertical loom in the New Kingdom, following the Hyksos invasion. At this time, it also became common for garments to be more elaborately pleated.

Aside from linen, animal-skin loincloths may have sometimes been worn, and following the introduction of wool-bearing sheep during the Middle Kingdom, wool was used to manufacture shawls that were worn on cold nights. Silk arrived later with the Greeks, but cotton remained unknown until Coptic times.

Most Egyptians probably went barefoot much of the time, but before the introduction of shoes during the New Kingdom, open-toed sandals, made from reeds, leather, or a combination of the two, were also worn.

Items of jewelry, such as rings, earrings, and bangles were commonplace, as were amulets, which were worn to ward off evil and bring good luck.

Hair and Make-up

Children in Ancient Egypt wore their hair shaved except for a pigtail to one side, which was known as "the sidelock of youth." Adults, meanwhile, either shaved their heads (as well as facial and body hair), or grew their hair; short for men and longer for women. It was also customary for both sexes to wear wigs, make-up, and scented oils, which apart from enhancing the appearance and providing pleasant odors, also offered protection from the sun, sand and insects, and were also believed to have medicinal and magical properties. Smells were often given religious associations, and as bad smells were associated with sin and impurity, oils and incense were used to mask body odors. Most of the oils and incense used by the Egyptians was imported from the Middle East, and in fact, after timber, was the main reason for trade.

Various minerals were used to produce make-up, including green malachite and ground black galena, or soot, which were used to produce kohl for the eyes. Red ochre or iron oxide was used to make lipstick and rouge, and nails were also painted. Hair was often dyed with henna.

Left: Gold bracelet with a lapis lazuli scarab from the tomb of Amenemope. Egyptian jewelers had access to many semiprecious stones from the deserts and also imported light blue turquoise and rich blue lapis lazuli from other countries such as Sinai and Afghanistan.

Opposite: Wall painting from the 18th Dynasty tomb of Pere, depicting the tomb owner and his wife before an altar laden with offerings. Courtiers often tied cones of scented animal fat to their wigs, sometimes with a lotus blossom. The fat would melt and slide down the wig, keeping them cool and sweet-smelling.

Trade and the Economy

Egypt was the wealthiest country of the ancient world, but until the Late Period it operated a nonmonetary economy. A barter system was used for both domestic and foreign trade. Wages and taxes were also paid in produce. At its simplest level this system involved two parties adding to or removing goods to be bartered until each was satisfied and a deal was struck. The vendor may or may not have wanted what he took in exchange. In the latter case he would have wanted to insure that the goods received could be used in a future transaction. This was an unwieldy system and by the New Kingdom—possibly earlier—a transaction system based on copper weights was introduced for low-value items, with silver and gold used for more expensive goods.

Egypt was largely self-sufficient but it did look beyond its shores for certain goods: cedarwood from Lebanon; lapis lazuli from Afghanistan; ebony and ivory from central Africa; silver and bronze from Syria; olive oil from Crete. Egypt's large gold reserves were often used for exchange purposes.

Particularly at the height of the country's imperial power, goods were often received as diplomatic gifts or tribute. The first coinage appeared during the 25th Dynasty, c. 400 BC, the precursor to the introduction of a full monetary economy during the Ptolemaic Period.

Weights and Measure

Although it seems that the Ancient Egyptians did not fully understand true multiplication and division, and could probably not conceive of mathematics in abstract terms, they possessed a decimal system for counting, were able to calculate area with some accuracy, created the earliest known clocks, and also established the basis of the calendar that we use to this day.

It is thought that the Egyptian decimal system was developed during the early part of the Old Kingdom, and

Below: Wall painting from the tomb of the 18th Dynasty official Nebamun at Thebes. In this scene cattle are paraded before the tomb owner, while elsewhere geese are counted to assess Nebamun's wealth. An important part of a person's wealth was the number of cattle he owned.

There was no real monetary system in Ancient Egypt until coins were introduced around 400 BC, but prior to this, goods were given a nominal value in deben weights of metal and stone, which were sometimes shaped like animals.

The Calendar

The Egyptian calendar was based on astronomical observations, and the year began with the rising of the Dog-star, Sirius or Sothis, and was divided into twelve months, each of thirty days, with five extra holy days, providing the first 365-day year. Each month was divided into three weeks of ten days, and each day into twenty-four hours, although not all of these hours were the same length! Time was measured with shadow clocks or sundials, and also with water clocks: stone vessels with a hole in the bottom through which water escaped, with a scale inscribed on the inside that marked the passing of the hours as the water level fell.

it consisted of different symbols which represented the numbers 1, 10, 100, and so on, with each symbol being repeated as required to denote a given number. Thus, the number 7, for example, would be represented by repeating the symbol for 1 seven times. There was even a symbol for one million, but it is thought that this may have been used to suggest infinity, as opposed to being an exact value.

Length was measured according to standardized proportions of the body, with the principal measurement being the cubit, or the length of the forearm, which equated to about 21 inches, and for smaller measurements was divided into palm and thumb widths. Four cubits comprised a fathom, or the height of a man to his hairline, whilst longer distances were recorded in "river measures" of 20,000 cubits (around 6.8 miles).

The unit of area for measuring land was the aroura/setjat, which was equal to 100 square cubits, and the Egyptians are thought to have had an understanding of pi, which they calculated as 3.16 rather than 3.142, but which enabled them to work out the area of triangles and circles. Capacity was measured in hin, equal to around one pint, ten of which comprised one hektat.

The unit of weight was the deben, which was equivalent to approximately 3.2 oz, and the kite and sep were later introduced, with ten kites equal to one deben, and 100 kites equal to one sep, or ten deben.

Above: Fragment of a sunk relief showing scribes rendering accounts. Akhenaten's preoccupation with the cult of the Aten contributed toward a period of economic decline, which in turn caused internal disorder and a weakening of royal authority.

Below: Detail of a wall painting from the tomb of Panekhmen, depicting metalworkers weighing gold on scales.

Law and Order

Egyptian society was strictly ordered and governed by numerous departments, ministers, and officials, but ultimate power rested with the king or pharaoh, who from the time of the Fourth Dynasty onward was regarded as the living embodiment of the god Horus, the upholder of maat, and the dispenser of divine justice. Maat was the goddess of truth, morality, and justice, but it was also the name for the Egyptian concept of order and stability, which extended into moral conduct. Wrongdoing was therefore seen as being against maat, or the correct order of things. It appears that there was no definitive written law, rather an unwritten code of conduct based upon the judgment of the pharaohs, although court records were meticulously kept by scribes, and judgments would most likely have set precedents.

There were town and district courts, made up of respected citizens or local officials, but the most serious matters might be heard before the king's viziers, or even the pharaoh himself. Anyone accused of a crime could represent themselves in court, and was entitled to a fair hearing, although innocence was not always presumed before proof of guilt had been established, and suspects were often beaten. Beatings were also given as punishments, as was confiscation of property, branding, and the amputation of hands, ears, and noses. Sometimes people were also sent into exile or executed, but only the pharaoh could authorize a death sentence.

Order was initially enforced by officials and soldiers, but during the New Kingdom this role was mainly fullfilled by a tribe of Nubians known as the Medjay, who effectively became an official police force.

Right: A detail from the chariot of Tutankhamun. The falcon god Horus was associated with kingship: the pharaoh was regarded as a living embodiment of Horus and was therefore believed to be divine himself. He enforced the law in the name of Maat—the goddess of truth, morality and justice.

Settlements and Housing

The earliest Egyptian homes would have been very simple shelters constructed of bundles of reeds secured between wooden posts, but from the time of the Old Kingdom onward, all houses were constructed of mud bricks. These were made from a mixture of mud, straw, and stone, which was placed in a wooden mold and left to harden in the sun. Later during the New Kingdom, these bricks would have been fired in kilns.

The homes of the poorest people may have consisted of just one room, but most houses would have had two or more rooms, including a living room, which was also used for eating and sleeping, small storerooms, and a small open-air yard or cooking area, from which stairs or a ladder would have led to a flat roof terrace, where families would sleep on very hot nights. The houses of the more wealthy may have been raised off the ground, had up to four stories, contained separate sleeping areas, and been decoratively painted inside, whilst the most affluent and important people, such as officials, lived in villas with a large, central living area surrounded by as many as twenty smaller rooms. These homes often had courtyard gardens containing trees, vegetable and flower

beds, and even fishponds. Most townhouses, however, were packed closely together in terraces along a narrow central street.

Houses were whitewashed to seal the walls and reflect heat, and had just one or two small windows, which were usually north-facing and placed high up, to benefit from the breeze and avoid the full heat of the sun, but they would have been quite dark inside, and linseed oil lamps were used to provide light.

Most homes were very sparsely furnished, with simple wooden items such as beds, low stools and tables, baskets and boxes, and only the wealthy would have possessed items such as chairs, which in some cases may have been constructed from imported woods and decorated with precious metals and stones.

Below: Vignette from the Book of the Dead showing Nakht, an 18th Dynasty scribe and astronomer, with his wife Tawi. The picture shows their white-painted house (far right) and a fishpond surrounded by trees on all sides.

Military Life, War, and Weaponry

Ancient Egypt was well protected by the natural defenses provided by the surrounding deserts and the Mediterranean Sea, and during the Old Kingdom there was no real professional army, only the king's bodyguards, and local bands of trained conscripts that could be called upon to defend Egypt's borders when necessary. However, by the Middle Kingdom, the pharaohs had begun to establish fortresses in order to colonize Nubia to the south, and Nubian mercenaries soon began to join the Egyptians in battle.

Around 1670 BC, the Hyksos people of the Middle East invaded, taking control of the Nile Delta for around 100 years, following which, during the New Kingdom, the Egyptians established a professional standing army, and also began to expand their territories to the north and into the Middle East. The Hyksos also left a legacy of new weapons, such as the scimitar, improved armor, helmets, and horses and chariots, which further strengthened the Egyptian army.

The pharaoh, or sometimes his son, headed the army. As well as accompanying their forces on campaigns, kings may well have fought alongside them, and are often depicted as doing so in tomb paintings. The army was composed of divisions of 5000 men, each with 4000 infantry and 500 two-man chariots, which were further divided into companies of 200 infantry and 25 chariots. These companies were grouped in units of 50 infantry, who are thought to have specialized in the use of particular weapons, such as spears, slings, bows, swords, maces, axes, and daggers, whilst chariots contained a driver and either an archer or spear-thrower. Originally protection was offered only by wood and leather shields, but mailcoats were introduced during the New Kingdom, which consisted of bronze plates attached to leather jerkins.

The Egyptians routinely removed the hands of enemy dead to aid in counting how many they had killed, and battles were undoubtedly highly dangerous and

bloody affairs. Even in peacetime the life of a soldier was hard, for he would often be employed to labor on vast building projects, quarrying and mining, but there were also advantages. Soldiers made a fairly good living, and the most distinguished could expect to be honored with gold medals, other precious objects, and land, whilst conscripted slaves could also win their freedom.

Above: Preparatory drawing for a tomb relief depicting a horse and chariot.

Right: Detail from the wooden casket found in the antechamber of Tutankhamun's tomb, which bore exquisitely painted hunting and battle scenes. It shows the Nubians being crushed by the king. The jumble of bodies of the vanquished also suggests chaos, out of which Tutankhamun has brought order.

Opposite: Detail from the magnificent painted wooden casket found in Tutankhamun's tomb. It shows the horse-drawn chariot, which arrived in Egypt during the Second Intermediate Period, c. 1650—c. 1550 BC. As a fast-moving platform from which archers could fire their arrows, the chariot quickly became an important part of Egypt's military capability.

The Tombs

By the dawn of the New Kingdom, around 1550 BC, the age of pyramid building was long over. The pyramids had been looted of their funerary goods, and almost all of the New Kingdom pharaohs would instead be entombed in a remote valley at the edge of the desert opposite Thebes. This area would become known as the Valley of the Kings. Here, the Ancient Egyptians established a vast royal necropolis, with a series of magnificently decorated underground tombs cut deep into the valley, and a huge temple complex erected on the Theban plain. It was hoped that this site would offer a more secure resting place for the last great kings of Egypt and their treasures, but over time, these tombs would also fall victim to tomb robbers, and would eventually be abandoned. Even the tomb of Tutankhamun was looted, but it is as a result of the huge horde of treasures that remained to be unearthed from his tomb in 1922 by Howard Carter that Tutankhamun and the Valley of the Kings have become so well known, and continue to capture the imagination to this day.

Why Thebes?

There are thought to be several reasons, both practical and symbolic, why this area of Western Thebes was chosen for the New Kingdom necropolis. The site is close to the city of Thebes, which had become both the religious and administrative capital of Egypt with a flat plain that was an ideal location for the construction of mortuary temples, beyond which a large ravine sheltered the isolated valley, with its numerous smaller ravines and coves. In theory, the Valley of the Kings could only be reached by two pathways, and so could be easily guarded.

Left: The arid Valley of the Kings is situated on the west bank of the River Nile. Its proximity to the city of Thebes and many coves made it an ideal site for the royal necropolis.

It was also important that the site be located on the west bank of the Nile; being the place where the sun set and, it was believed, began its journey through the Underworld, it was closely associated with the Egyptian idea of death and rebirth. Additionally, when seen from Thebes, the cliffs in front of the Valley of the Kings closely resembled the shape of the hieroglyph for "horizon": a solar disk rising or setting between two mountains.

A further symbolic element may be found in the fact that the valley is situated in the shadow of al-Qurn, or "The Lady of the Peak": a hill topped with a natural pyramid.

Early Tombs at Thebes

The first pharaoh known to have been entombed in the Valley of the Kings was Tuthmosis I, the third ruler of the 18th Dynasty. However, areas nearby had been in use as royal burial grounds since the First Intermediate Period, when the Theban rulers Intef (Inyotef) I, II, and III were buried in saff tombs at el-Tarif. These were cut directly into the rock face, with pillared entrances that led to a chapel, before a long shaft descended to a burial chamber. The

first pharaoh of the Middle Kingdom, King Mentuhotep I, is also thought to have been buried in this kind of tomb, beneath his mortuary temple at Deir el-Bahri on the Theban Plain, just in front of the Valley of the Kings. However, it was not until after the end of the Second Intermediate Period, when the Thebans had successfully driven out the Hyksos invaders, who had occupied Egypt for 100 years, that Thebes would be restored as the Egyptian capital, and the Theban necropolis and the Valley of the Kings would become Egypt's most sacred site.

Tomb Designs and Developments

The royal tombs at the Valley of the Kings have certain features in common, which are unlike those of any tombs previously constructed, particularly in their location and in being so richly decorated with wall paintings. While all are also unique in their individual design and construction, they can generally be categorized into three main types, roughly according to the dynasty during which they were constructed, demonstrating a series of developments in terms of their location, layout, size, and decoration.

Throughout much of the 18th Dynasty tombs were usually cut into the cliff walls, and consisted of a series of steep, stepped and sloping passageways, which led first to a well shaft that was designed to prevent flooding and deter robbers, before opening on to a pillared hall, and a further passage that led to the burial chamber itself. These early tombs typically followed a winding path, with a change of direction at the first pillared hall that is thought to have echoed the twisting path taken through the Underworld. This is reflected in inscriptions and decoration found in the burial chambers. The tomb of Tuthmosis III is thought to be the first to include a well chamber, the ceiling of which was decorated, and also decoration in the pillared hall, whilst that of Amenhotep (Amenophis) II saw the addition of a room at the bottom of the well and the division of the burial chamber into two parts; features that would be continued in many subsequent tombs.

From the late 18th Dynasty and throughout much of the next, tombs tended to be positioned in the lower slopes of the valley at the base of the cliffs, and saw a change from a twisting or right-angled plan, to a straighter layout, albeit with the second part of the tomb offset from the main axis at the first pillared hall. This was first seen in the tomb of Horemheb, as was much more precise cutting of the tomb's passageways, but the best example is undoubtedly the tomb of Seti (Sethos) I which is longer, deeper and more finished than any other tomb in the Valley of the Kings, and is also the first to have been decorated in its entirety. Interestingly, the burial chamber has a vaulted ceiling, which for the first time is decorated with astronomical designs.

The next major development, which would set a precedent for the remaining tombs of the 19th and 20th Dynasties, and is first seen in the tomb of Merneptah, is a completely straight axis from the entrance to the burial chamber. During this period tombs became simpler and smaller in plan, and also less steep, with those of Setnakhte and the later Ramessid tombs being almost horizontal in most cases. These tombs tended to be cut at ground level into rocky outcrops projecting from the cliffs and were less prone to flooding, but whilst wells were no longer excavated, the well room was retained. Perhaps most significantly, however, the sarcophagi in these tombs were realigned along the axis of the tomb instead of being perpendicular to it, which is thought to reflect the increasing focus on sun worship during this period, as does much of the decoration in these later tombs.

Right: Detail from Nefertari's tomb showing a falcon and an egret. The ruling pharaoh was believed to be the reincarnation of the god Horus who was represented in the form of a hawk.

Opposite: A banqueting scene from the tomb of Nebamun.

Above: Detail of a wall painting from the Theban tomb of Userhet, showing gifts of food provided by Hathor.

The Decline of the Necropolis, and the Royal Caches

The last known tomb to be constructed in the Valley of the Kings is that of Ramesses XI, the last ruler of the 20th Dynasty, but it is thought that his mummified remains were never buried there, most likely as a result of the large-scale plundering of the tombs that took place at the end of the 20th Dynasty, as documented in the "Tomb Robbery Papyri," which indicate that security in the Valley of the Kings could no longer be maintained. In fact, records show that several tombs had been completely ransacked during the reign of Ramesses IX.

Therefore, in an attempt to salvage valuable funerary goods and in order to protect the remaining royal mummies, the tombs were officially opened during the 21st Dynasty by the High Priests at Thebes and their contents were removed. However, it also seems that during this period of increasing social unrest, the priests at Thebes took to plundering the tombs of their goods with a view to boosting the failing economy.

The mummies themselves were rewrapped and transferred to two main caches. The first, which was discovered in AD 1881, represents the most significant number of mummies ever found, with forty being recovered from a tomb located high in the hills at Deir el-Bahri, which is thought to have been the intended family tomb of the king-priest Pinudjem II. The second cache was discovered in 1898, by Egyptologist Victor Loret in the tomb of the 18th Dynasty king Amenhotep (Amenophis) II, and consisted of sixteen mummies.

Many of the mummies have since been identified through inscriptions and dockets that were placed with them when they were rewrapped, and the caches are believed to include most of the New Kingdom pharaohs. However, it is thought possible that a third group may yet be discovered.

During the Late Dynastic Period, mummies were sometimes buried in the existing royal tombs, but until the discovery of Tutankhamun in 1922, Amenhotep (Amenophis) II was the only royal mummy to have been found in his own tomb.

Left: Wall painting from the tomb of Horemheb, a former army commander who rose to become a senior official during Tutankhamun's reign, and eventually pharaoh. A tomb had been prepared for Horemheb at Saqqara, but following his accession to the throne this was abandoned in favor of a more exalted resting place in the Valley of the Kings.

Tombs of the Nobles

Since the Early Dynastic Period, a tradition had been established whereby high-ranking officials and respected courtiers were often buried close to their masters, and this tradition was continued during the New Kingdom, with a number of nobles being interred in the Valley of the Kings, typically in tombs alongside those of the pharaohs they served.

As might be expected, these tombs were generally far less complex than most of the royal tombs, usually consisting of a single chamber that was reached by means of a vertical shaft, but there are some, referred to as "staircase tombs," that are closer in design to the royal tombs, with enlarged burial chambers, corridors, and stairways. However, these tombs were, almost without exception, far less ornate than the royal tombs. Decoration tended to focus on aspects of everyday life, rather than depictions of the gods, and the tombs also contained less extravagant funerary goods.

Most are thought to date from the 18th Dynasty, and as with almost all the tombs in the Valley of the Kings, they have been disturbed at various times since their construction, by tomb robbers, by being used as storerooms when new tombs were being cut or royal mummies were restored, and by being reused as family tombs after the end of the New Kingdom.

Despite this, several artifacts have been recovered from amongst the debris encountered in these tombs, including funerary equipment and mummies. In 1905 the Egyptologist James E. Quibell unearthed what would be one of the most significant finds until the discovery of King Tutankhamun's tomb: the tomb of Yuja and Tjuyu, the parents of Queen Tiye, who had been chief wife of Amenhotep III.

Right: 19th Dynasty tomb at Deir el-Medina, showing Pashedu, a member of the workforce that built the Valley of the Kings, drinking from a pool in the shade of a date palm.

Above: Wall painting from the tomb of Queen Nefertari in the Valley of the Queens, showing the union of the gods Re and Osiris, the latter depicted in the form of a ram.

The Valley of the Queens

Despite its name, the Valley of the Kings was not exclusively designated for the tombs of the male pharaohs, as a number of royal family members, including wives and children of the kings, were also buried in the area, as were high-ranking nobles. Additionally, the female pharaohs of the New Kingdom, Queen Hatshepsut, wife of Tuthmosis II, and Queen Twosret (Tawosret), wife of Sethos (Seti) II, had tombs constructed for them in the valley. However, from the start of the Nineteenth Dynasty, under King Ramesses I, a new burial site was established to the south of the Valley of the Kings, where his wife Queen Sitre was interred, and where many of the wives and children of the pharaohs would subsequently be buried. In ancient times it was named "Ta-Set-Neferu," meaning "the place of the children of the Pharaoh," but today it is known as the Valley of the Queens.

The site was excavated to some extent during the eighteenth century AD, but it was not until 1903 that more extensive exploration was undertaken, under the leadership of the Italian Egyptologist Ernesto Schiaparelli, who was the director of the Egyptian Museum in Turin. Around eighty tombs and burial pits have been discovered at the Valley of the Queens, which are now known to have been the last resting places of numerous queens, princes, and princesses. As in the Valley of the Kings, many of the tombs had been looted and badly damaged in ancient times, but several still contained highly lavish decoration, in the form of wall reliefs and paintings, including the tombs of Khaemwese (Khaemwaset) and Amenhikhopeshef, sons of Ramsses III, which contain paintings depicting them being presented to the gods with their father.

The most spectacular tomb, however, is that of Nefertari, chief wife of Ramesses II, which was discovered by Schiaparelli in 1904, and is widely acclaimed as one of

The tomb had been disturbed and robbed of almost all its smaller items, but the mummies of Yuja and Tjuyu were found to be in a remarkable state of preservation, and the tomb yielded an extraordinary array of burial goods, including large, ornate coffin canopies, mummiform coffins, canopic chests complete with jars containing mummified organs, several shabtis, a mirror, sandals, numerous vessels and jars, inlaid boxes, chairs, beds, and even a chariot.

the most beautiful tombs in Egypt. In fact, even in ancient times it was known as "Set Neferu," meaning "seat of beauty."

The tomb is painted throughout with probably the best-preserved and most lavish decorations of any tomb, which depict Nefertari in both life and in death, and follow her complete journey through the Underworld to the point of her rebirth into eternity. Interestingly, there are also inscriptions of poetry apparently written for her by her husband, and numerous references that reflect the unusually high position that she held in Egyptian society, such as "Hereditary Princess," "Great King's Wife" and "Lady of the Two Lands."

Right: Detail from the tomb of Sennedjem at Deir el-Medina, the village which housed the workers who built the Valley of the Kings. Sennedjem's tomb was discovered, perfectly preserved, in 1886.

Below: Detail from the banqueting scene from Nebamun's tomb in the Valley of the Nobles, showing one of the guests offering lotus blossom to the nose of another. The lotus was an important symbol of regeneration, and thus highly apposite as a funerary image.

Tutankhamun

Today, Tutankhamun is probably the name most associated with Ancient Egypt, on account of the excitement and interest aroused by the discovery of his tomb by Howard Carter and Lord Carnarvon in 1922. It is the most intact royal burial site of a New Kingdom pharaoh ever discovered, and the wealth of funerary goods, in terms of both quality and quantity, is outstanding. Additionally, while Tutankhamun's mummified remains are not the most well preserved example ever found, his was the only royal mummy of the New Kingdom known to have remained undisturbed in its tomb for some 3000 years.

However, while much has been learned from the discovery, a great deal about the reign of this short-lived and relatively minor pharaoh remains a mystery, and may never be fully understood.

The Boy King

Tutankhamun is thought to have been the only son of the 18th Dynasty pharaoh Amenhotep IV, or Akhenaten, as he renamed himself. During his reign, Egypt was subjected to enforced monotheism, or the worship of a single god which had sent the country into a state of both religious and social upheaval. It was against this backdrop that Tutankhamun ascended the throne, around 1333 BC, at the age of just eight or nine. This followed the incredibly brief reign of Smenkhkare, whom some have suggested was actually Akhenaten's wife Nefertiti. Tutankhamun's mother is considered to have been another of Akhenaten's wives, Kiya, who is believed to have died before her son was installed as king.

With no close female relatives, it is thought that the young successor was placed in the care of two high-ranking officials, Ay and Horemheb, who, acting as advisors to the boy king, were undoubtedly the real power behind the pharaoh, at least for several years. They appear to have seized the opportunity to condemn Tutankhamun's father Akhenaten as a heretic as well as restore power to the Theban priesthood and some semblance of harmony to Egypt. Interestingly, both would succeed to the throne following Tutankhamun's seemingly untimely death.

Perhaps tellingly, Tutankhamun was crowned at Memphis, rather than Akhetaten at el-Amarna, the capital that had been established by his father, and during his reign there would be a return to polytheism, or the worship of many gods, with Thebes being restored as the religious capital, and Amun as the most important of the cult deities. This was marked in the second year of the pharaoh's reign, with a change of name from Tutankhaten, as he was then known, meaning "Living image of the Aten," to Tutankhamun, or "Living image of the Amun." Despite this, following the pharaoh's sudden death at the age of about seventeen to nineteen, Horemheb seems to have attempted to obliterate the names of the Amarna Kings, Tutankhamun, Smenkhkare, and Akhenaten, from history.

Right: One of a number of magnificent pectorals recovered from Tutankhamun's tomb. The straps are formed from inlaid plaques with uraei, scarabs and solar disks. The pendant consists of a scarab holding the sun aloft, flanked by two uraei. The uraeus, or cobra, was associated with kingship and featured in most royal headdresses.

Opposite: The stunning mask which was made to cover Tutankhamun's mummy was made from gold and inlaid with precious stones and paste.

Above: A scene from the north wall of Tutankhamun's burial chamber, showing Ay, clad in the leopard skin of the sem priest, performing the Opening of the Mouth ceremony on the dead king.

Below: Detail of the golden shrine found in the antechamber of Tutankhamun's tomb. It was adorned with numerous delicate reliefs showing scenes of the royal couple's daily life.

Opposite: Panel from the back of the golden throne of Tutankhamun, showing Queen Ankhesenamun offering her husband perfume or ointment from a salve-cup.

There has been a great deal of speculation concerning Tutankhamun's death, particularly as injuries that were revealed upon examination of his mummy have suggested that he may have been murdered, or met an otherwise violent end, possibly as the result of a chariot accident. However, further examinations, including X-rays and CAT scans, have proved inconclusive.

Howard Carter and Lord Carnarvon

Howard Carter was born in London in 1874, the son of an artist and illustrator, and it was by initially following a similar path that he would eventually make the discovery of Tutankhamun's tomb. Carter had no formal education but his artistic ability was noted at a young age, leading the Egyptologist Percy Newbury to employ him, at the age of seventeen, to ink tracings of tomb interiors that had been brought from Egypt.

Still only seventeen, Carter was soon offered a position as an artist for the Egypt Exploration Fund, and made his first visit to the country, where he was to spend six years drawing tomb scenes and assisting with excavations. By 1899, Carter had achieved the position of "Chief Inspector of Antiquities for Upper Egypt," working under Gaston Maspero for the Directorate of the Egyptian Service des Antiquités, a position he would hold until 1904, and in this role, he gained experience in excavating tombs in the Valley of the Kings, made notable contributions to restoring several of them, and introduced electric lighting to the best of them. However, in 1904, Carter was transferred to the northern Inspectorate, and the following year would resign from the Service des Antiquités after an argument with tourists at Saqqara.

Carter worked as an independent artist until 1907, when he was hired by Lord Carnarvon, a wealthy patron with an interest in Egyptology. The two began excavations at various sites, until in 1915 Carter was presented with the opportunity of returning to the Valley of the Kings. Many felt that the Valley had yielded all that it had to offer, but a number of small finds by various Egyptologists in the intervening years, such as a faience cup, embalming materials, and several fragments of gold that bore the inscription of Tutankhamun, had convinced Carter otherwise.

Working for Carnarvon, Carter began his excavations in 1917, but by 1922 he had found little further evidence of the tomb he was so desperately searching for, and a disheartened Carnarvon was ready to call off the search and withdraw his funding. However, Carter managed to persuade him to persevere for one more season.

The Discovery of the Tomb

On November 4, 1922, just days after Carter had begun his excavations, he discovered a step cut into the rock close to the entrance of the tomb of Ramesses VI, and further excavation would reveal a flight of sixteen steps that descended to a doorway, closed with the "Jackal-and-Nine-Captives" seal of the necropolis guards. No royal seal was yet apparent, but Carter immediately dispatched a telegram to Carnarvon and awaited his arrival.

Carnarvon arrived at the scene on November 23, and work was quickly resumed. The temporary infill that Carter had put in place was excavated, and in the process, the seal of Tutankhamun was revealed to them for the first time at the base of the door, but the men also realized that the door had been opened and resealed twice before. Beyond the door, a rubble-filled, sloping corridor was cleared, and a second sealed doorway became visible. Carter made a small hole, large enough through which to insert a candle, and looked inside.

"Wonderful Things"

Peering into the darkness, Carter was apparently stunned by what he took in as his eyes adjusted to the candlelight, and he would later recount that what he saw was: "everywhere the glint of gold…," and when Carnarvon asked, "Can you see anything?" he replied, "Yes, wonderful things."

Entering the tomb, into the Antechamber, they were confronted by a vast array of objects, over 700 in all, which included cups, vases, and other vessels,

Left: Hunting scene from one of the chests found in Tutankhamun's tomb, showing the king in action, with Queen Ankhesenamun looking on. Many objects recovered from the chests were associated with such manly pursuits befitting an Egyptian ruler. These included slings, clubs, boomerangs, throw-sticks, swords, and archery equipment.

funerary paraphernalia, all of which required careful removal and cataloguing before Carter could advance farther into the tomb.

Once the Antechamber had been emptied, Carter cleared the doorway to the burial chamber, and was confronted by what initially appeared to be a wall of gold. However, this was revealed to be one of four gilded wooden shrines, each contained within the other, that almost completely occupied the burial chamber. These were painstakingly removed, to reveal a huge quartzite sarcophagus with a red granite top, and a further room beyond, which Carter named the Treasury. This was guarded by a statue of the jackal-god Anubis, atop a wooden shrine, and against the far wall, amongst several smaller caskets and boxes, stood a huge gilded shrine. This housed the canopic chest, containing the canopic jars in which the mummified liver, lungs, stomach, and intestines of the pharaoh had been placed.

Carter removed the lid of the stone sarcophagus in 1924, and was stunned by the magnificence of its contents. It contained three anthropomorphic or mummiform coffins, placed one inside the other, the first two of which were of gilded wood, the second being ornately decorated with faience and semiprecious stones, whilst the third was made of solid gold. This was opened to reveal Tutankhamun's mummified body, adorned with a solid gold mask. Carter unwrapped the mummy, to find over 170 amulets placed within the layers of fabric, intended to provide safe passage to the afterlife. Unfortunately, however, it seems that the mummy itself was relatively poorly preserved, possibly as a result of over-anointing, but it now seems likely, too, that Carter was rather less careful with the body than he recorded in his reports, and he is thought to have contributed to its damage.

inlaid and painted boxes and caskets, clothing, cosmetics, figurines, musical instruments, writing implements, weaponry, shrines, couches, chairs, beds, and the parts of several chariots. To the right was another doorway, guarded by two life-size figures of the pharaoh, beyond which, Carter was sure, lay the burial chamber. Directly ahead was the Annexe, containing more furniture and

Above: A pendant from the tomb of Tutankhamun. The king's mummy was decorated with over 150 pieces of jewelry.

Left: Perfume jar from Tutankhamun's burial chamber. Although the king was interred with many magnificent pieces, and the tomb was the best preserved of any discovered thus far, the burial chamber itself was small.

The Tomb, its Decoration, and the King's Burial

Although some provision had already been made for Tutankhamun's burial, as can be seen by the fact that the inner and outer coffins and gold mask bore his likeness, the tomb itself and many of the funerary items contained within suggest that his death was sudden and unexpected. The tomb itself is too small to have been intended for royal use, and was probably extended after his death in an attempt to provide room for the vast array of possessions that were interred with him, and to provide a more fitting resting place for a king. It seems likely that this tomb was actually intended for Tutankhamun's advisor Ay, who was eventually buried in that which was originally planned for the pharaoh.

Several of the artifacts in the tomb, such as one of the shrines, the mummiform coffinettes contained within the canopic chest, and the middle of the three coffins, are thought to have been made for Smenkhkare, Tutankhamun's predecessor, and altered texts on the sarcophagus box suggest that it was also originally intended for someone else, most likely because preparations for the pharaoh's burial had to be made within the seventy days allocated for the embalming process.

As was common during the 18th Dynasty, only the burial chamber was decorated, however; there are some unusual depictions that would be more befitting the tomb of a noble or the private tomb of a wealthy citizen than that of a king, such as the image of the funerary cortège painted on the east wall. The south and west walls bear images of the king being welcomed to the Underworld, along with twelve baboons that represent the hours of the night, whilst the north wall shows more images of Tutankhamun embraced by the gods. However, it is also painted with the Opening of the Mouth ceremony, which is otherwise unknown in royal tombs, and what is more, Ay is depicted performing the ceremony, as if to legitimize his claim to the throne.

Below: A detail of the gilt shrine of Tutankhamun which originally contained statuettes of the royal couple. It depicts a ritual hunting scene in which Queen Ankhesenamun helps her husband.

The Pharaohs

From the time of the unification of Upper and Lower Egypt by King Narmer around 3100 BC, until the end of the reign of the last native Egyptian king, Nakhthoreb, or Nectanebo II, about 343 BC, Ancient Egypt was ruled by a succession of approximately 170 kings, and a handful of queens, whom we know as "pharaohs," a Greek word, which is thought to derive from the Egyptian "per-aa," meaning "great house." This is a reference to the royal palace, but by the time of the New Kingdom, the term had become an accepted means of referring to the king himself.

Throughout its approximately 3000-year history, the civilization of Ancient Egypt was essentially governed as a theocracy, that is to say, by a priesthood, with the pharaoh holding absolute and divine power. The pharaoh was not thought of as merely a representative of the gods, but from the time of their coronation with the shemty, or "Double Crown of the Two Lands," as the actual embodiment of the gods on Earth, to whom the entire population was subservient.

As well as being the religious head of state, the pharaoh was in charge of government, the law courts and the military, and ultimately was deemed to own all of the land, property, and people of Egypt. As such, most of the pharaohs commanded incredible wealth and power, as testified by the vast monuments that were erected in their honour.

However, whilst the pharaohs were believed to be divine and without equal on Earth, they were typically visible amongst their people, and often performed important duties, such as laying foundation stones at temples, in person. The pharaoh was also expected to uphold the principles of maat, or justice, and had a responsibility to his people, for it was his governance that would decide their fate, and his duty to rejoin the gods at death in order that the people of Egypt could continue to prosper.

Narmer — Early Dynastic Period

According to Manetho's "Aegyptiaca," the civilization of Ancient Egypt begins around 3100 BC with the unification of Upper and Lower Egypt, or the "Two Lands," under one ruler. However, there remains some confusion as to exactly who this ruler was, and the history and chronology of the early kings of Egypt is far from clear. Whilst "Menes" appears as the first name in Manetho's list of dynasties, two other names appear in records of the Early Dynastic Period: "Narmer" and "Hor-Aha." Some historians propose that Hor-Aha was Narmer's son and successor, whilst others suggest that Menes, Narmer, and Hor-Aha may have been one and the same person. Although the precise facts may never be fully established, the earliest artifact that depicts a king of both Upper and Lower Egypt bears Narmer's name. This is the Narmer Palette, an inscribed cosmetic scoop of green slate that shows Narmer wearing the White Crown of Upper Egypt on one side and the Red Crown of Lower Egypt on the other. These are

Left: One of the most important artifacts relating to the Early Dynastic Period is the Narmer Palette. This tablet shows Narmer bearing the same ceremonial crown as Scorpion, one of the last kings of the Protodynastic Period.

in order to keep the Bedouin tribes under control and enable the mining of turquoise. Despite his remarkable achievements, however, and the fact that his funerary cult would be perpetuated for almost 2000 years, until the last native royal dynasty, in literature that was written after his reign Khufu is often represented as a cruel tyrant. Stories tell of the pharaoh's ruthlessness toward the Egyptian people, and even his own family, as he attempted to guarantee the successful completion of the Great Pyramid and the survival of his dynasty.

Mentuhotep I — 11th Dynasty

Following the breakdown of the Old Kingdom, Egypt entered a period of disunity and instability that would last for about 100 years. This is known as the First Intermediate Period, and was a time when there were internal rivalries in Egypt between provincial governors, or nomarchs, and no one king held overall control of the country. However, this period was brought to a close with the foundation of the 11th Dynasty by Mentuhotep I, under which Egypt was

accompanied by scenes of conquest, which probably refer to his victories in the north of the country that led to the unification of Egypt and the subsequent foundation of Memphis as the capital city.

Khufu — 4th Dynasty

Although he was not the first pharaoh to construct a pyramid—that distinction being credited to King Djoser of the Third Dynasty—Khufu, or Cheops, as the Greeks would later name him, was responsible for the construction of the Great Pyramid at Giza, which was the largest pyramid ever constructed, and the only one of the Seven Wonders of the Ancient World that still stands to this day. Inscriptions reveal that granite used in the construction of the pyramid was quarried far to the south at Aswan, whilst others indicate that Khufu's activities elsewhere included sending troops to Nubia, and also to the Sinai Peninsula, probably

Above: The three pyramids at Giza are tombs for Khufu, his son Khafra, and his grandson Menkaure. Khafra's pyramid appears larger than Khufu's Great Pyramid beyond it, an illusion created by the fact that it was built on higher ground.
Right: Fragment of the temple wall of Mentuhotep II.

reunited. Some historians credit the achievement of reunification to his successor Mentuhotep II, the first ruler of the Middle Kingdom, whilst other sources suggest that they may have been the same person. The first part of Mentuhotep's reign was characterized by conflict, including military campaigns to Nubia and Palestine to regain control of territories that had been lost during the First Intermediate Period, but following reunification, which was achieved in part by combining Amun and Re, the main gods of Upper and Lower Egypt, as Amun-Re, the country entered a phase of peace and stability that witnessed the initiation of numerous building projects, including Mentuhotep's impressive mortuary temple-tomb at Deir el-Bahri, on the west bank of the Nile opposite Thebes.

Senusret III — 12th Dynasty

Senusret III is thought to have been the most powerful pharaoh of the Middle Kingdom, and is regarded as both a great warrior and statesman. He is also believed to have been unusually large with an imposing physical presence. Manetho documents his height as four cubits, three palms and two fingers, equating to over six feet six inches tall. Senusret III introduced reforms that diminished the power of the regional nomarchs by establishing three major administrative districts, and in so doing secured Egypt's internal stability. With this achieved, he was able to direct his attentions to strengthening the country's borders, suppressing attacks by foreign invaders and maintaining

routes by which trade took place and minerals were obtained. Most of his campaigns were fought against the Nubians, and he extended the southern borders of Egypt farther than any previous pharaoh, defending them by the construction of a series of forts. He also cut a canal at the First Cataract at Aswan, facilitating the movement of troops and goods to and from the south. With the wealth gained from his military activities, Senusret III was able to restore a number of temples and initiate new building projects, including his pyramid at Dahshur.

Hatshepsut — 18th Dynasty

The foundation of the New Kingdom, which marked a return to stability in Egypt following the Second Intermediate Period, began with the expulsion of the

Above: Relief from Karnak, showing Hatshepsut, in masculine form, being crowned by Amun. The hieroglyphs relating to Amun were defaced during Akhenaten's reign and restored later.

Left: Hatshepsut's funerary temple at Deir el-Bahri. After a seven-year period as regent for her stepson Tuthmosis III, Hapshepsut proclaimed herself pharaoh.

occupying Hyksos, and the establishment of the 18th Dynasty by Ahmose, a Dynasty that was to include some of the most famous of all the Egyptian pharaohs, not least Queen Hatshepsut, who was to become the most powerful female ruler in Egyptian history. Initially Hatshepsut ruled as coregent with her stepson, Tuthmosis III, who had succeeded to the throne but was too young to reign. However, she rapidly assumed power, and using propaganda to assert her position, became one of the most successful pharaohs, and the first female pharaoh to assume the title "King of Upper and Lower Egypt," Amongst her most significant achievements were a massive program of building works throughout Egypt, the re-establishment of numerous trade routes, and the initiation of expeditions to the far south, including a voyage to Punt, where she acquired several incense trees that were to be planted in front of her impressive mortuary temple at Deir el-Bahri. Following her death, this temple and many of her monuments were defaced, and even destroyed, acts that have generally been ascribed to a vengeful Tuthmosis III.

Tuthmosis III — 18th Dynasty

Although short in stature, as has been revealed by the discovery of his mummy, which is barely five feet tall, Tuthmosis III was an expansionist king and a mighty military leader, which have led some to describe him as "the Napoleon of Egypt." He ascended to the throne at about the age of twenty-three, following the death of his stepmother Hatshepsut, who had "usurped" his rule by assuming the role of pharaoh when he was an infant. However, there is little evidence to suggest that he sought to take back power while she was alive. After her death, Tuthmosis III continued to rule independently for around thirty years, during which time he is thought to have led at least seventeen campaigns, capturing as many as 350 cities from Nubia to the Euphrates, and he was the first pharaoh to cross that river, expanding Egypt's territory to its greatest extent. Furthermore, Tuthmosis III insured that captured foreign princes were educated in Egyptian customs before being returned home, and his harem included several foreign princesses, possibly for diplomatic reasons. In addition to his military achievements, Tuthmosis III was also a prolific monument and temple builder, notably erecting memorials that celebrated his military prowess and expanding the great temple complex of Karnak.

Above: One of two statues of Amenhotep III, which originally stood at the entrance to his mortuary temple. The statues are nearly sixty feet tall and made from sandstone.

Amenhotep III – 18th Dynasty

Amenhotep III enjoyed a reign of almost forty years, during which time Egypt experienced a period of previously unequaled prosperity, which was to bear witness to the flourishing of architecture and sculpture. The king is thought to have ascended to the throne as a child, and to have embarked on some minor military campaigns as a young man, but overall his tenure was characterized by peace, and the opulence that Egypt enjoyed was as a result of excellent foreign relations, trade, and the mining of gold. Amenhotep III oversaw extensive temple building projects, particularly at Karnak, and at Thebes, where his mortuary temple was constructed. Unfortunately, this was destroyed during the 19th Dynasty, probably by a combination of flooding and the later reclamation of stone by successive pharaohs. However, the famous Colossi of Memmon, two huge stone statues of the seated pharaoh, still remain where the temple once stood, although today they are severely worn and weathered. Amenhotep III's chief architect is one of the few that we know by name: Amenhotep son of Hapu, and he too was commemorated with fine statues. Amenhotep III fathered two sons with his chief wife, Tiye. The first, Tuthmosis, died prematurely, but his successor was Amenhotep IV, who would later be known as Akhenaten, the heretic.

Ramesses II – 19th Dynasty

Also known as "Ramesses the Great," Ramesses II is thought to have been Egypt's longest-reigning pharaoh, and probably one of the most long-lived, ruling for around sixty-six years, and supposedly reaching over ninety years of age. The son of King Seti I and Queen Tuya, Ramesses II became Prince Regent at about fourteen, and ascended to the throne at around the age of twenty-five, by which time he was no doubt well trained in the art of war. In about the

fifth year of his reign, Ramesses II mobilized a vast army against the Hittites at Kadesh, resulting in a celebrated, but ultimately inconclusive, battle which would be followed by several campaigns to Syria in subsequent years. Eventually, however, a peace accord was drawn up—the earliest known document of its kind—and Ramesses II accepted two Hittite princesses, daughters of King Hattusili III, as wives. Aside from his military exploits, like many of the great pharaohs, Ramesses II is also well remembered for his monument building, and he was one of the most prolific pharaohs in this regard. His legacy includes his huge mortuary temple at Thebes, known as the Ramesseum, and his rock-cut temple at Abu Simbel, which is fronted by four vast seated figures of the king himself.

Cleopatra

The last ruler of the Ptolemaic line was Egypt's most famous queen, Cleopatra VII. Despite the mythology that grew to surround her, Cleopatra does not appear to have been a ravishing beauty. She was certainly politically astute and intellectually gifted, skills she employed to the maximum to secure power for herself and her children, an attempt which ended in failure and suicide.

Cleopatra ruled as coregent with her father, Ptolemy XII, and thereafter with her brother, Ptolemy XIII, whom she also married. Ousted from power by Ptolemy XIII in 48 BC, Cleopatra temporarily removed to Syria. When the Roman consul Pompey fled to Egypt following defeat by Julius Caesar in the Battle of Pharsalia, Cleopatra used the situation to her advantage. Pompey had been appointed her guardian in the wake of her father's death. Following his assassination by members of the Egyptian court, Cleopatra appealed to the victorious Caesar, who had pursued Pompey to Egypt. Caesar restored her to the throne, and when Ptolemy XIII was drowned in the Nile during a skirmish with Roman soldiers, Cleopatra ruled alongside her second brother, Ptolemy XIV, whom she also married.

Cleopatra and Caesar—some thirty years her senior—became lovers, and a year later, 47 BC, she bore him a child, Ptolemy Caesarion. She accompanied Caesar to Rome in 46 BC,

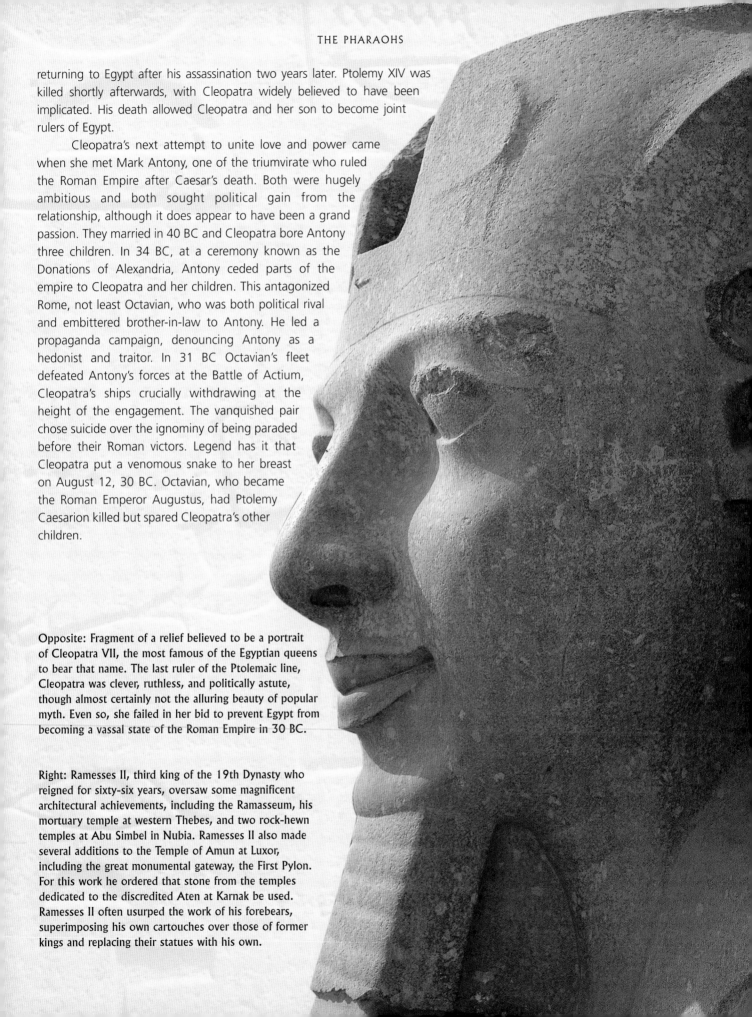

returning to Egypt after his assassination two years later. Ptolemy XIV was killed shortly afterwards, with Cleopatra widely believed to have been implicated. His death allowed Cleopatra and her son to become joint rulers of Egypt.

Cleopatra's next attempt to unite love and power came when she met Mark Antony, one of the triumvirate who ruled the Roman Empire after Caesar's death. Both were hugely ambitious and both sought political gain from the relationship, although it does appear to have been a grand passion. They married in 40 BC and Cleopatra bore Antony three children. In 34 BC, at a ceremony known as the Donations of Alexandria, Antony ceded parts of the empire to Cleopatra and her children. This antagonized Rome, not least Octavian, who was both political rival and embittered brother-in-law to Antony. He led a propaganda campaign, denouncing Antony as a hedonist and traitor. In 31 BC Octavian's fleet defeated Antony's forces at the Battle of Actium, Cleopatra's ships crucially withdrawing at the height of the engagement. The vanquished pair chose suicide over the ignominy of being paraded before their Roman victors. Legend has it that Cleopatra put a venomous snake to her breast on August 12, 30 BC. Octavian, who became the Roman Emperor Augustus, had Ptolemy Caesarion killed but spared Cleopatra's other children.

Opposite: Fragment of a relief believed to be a portrait of Cleopatra VII, the most famous of the Egyptian queens to bear that name. The last ruler of the Ptolemaic line, Cleopatra was clever, ruthless, and politically astute, though almost certainly not the alluring beauty of popular myth. Even so, she failed in her bid to prevent Egypt from becoming a vassal state of the Roman Empire in 30 BC.

Right: Ramesses II, third king of the 19th Dynasty who reigned for sixty-six years, oversaw some magnificent architectural achievements, including the Ramasseum, his mortuary temple at western Thebes, and two rock-hewn temples at Abu Simbel in Nubia. Ramesses II also made several additions to the Temple of Amun at Luxor, including the great monumental gateway, the First Pylon. For this work he ordered that stone from the temples dedicated to the discredited Aten at Karnak be used. Ramesses II often usurped the work of his forebears, superimposing his own cartouches over those of former kings and replacing their statues with his own.

Bibliography

Ancient Egyptians
Anton Gill/HarperCollins

The British Museum Book of Ancient Egypt
Ed by Stephen Quirke & Jeffrey Spencer

The Complete Tutankhamun
Nicholas Reeves Thames & Hudson

Tutankhamen: The Life and Death of a Boy King
Christine el Mahdy/Headline

Ancient Egypt: The Great Discoveries
Nicholas Reeves/Thames & Hudson

Egypt: The World of the Pharaohs
Ed by Regine Schulz & Matthias Seidel/Konemann

British Museum Dictionary of Ancient Egypt
Ian Shaw and Paul Nicholson/BCA

Egypt: The Splendours of an Ancient Civilization
Alberto Sillotti/Thames & Hudson

Ancient Egypt
Lorna Oakes & Lucia Gahlin/Hermes House

Gods of Ancient Egypt
B Watterson/Sutton Publishing

Discovering Ancient Egypt
Rosalie David/Michael O'Mara Books Ltd

Egyptology
James Putnam/Grange Books

Ramesses: The Great Warrior and Builder
Bernadette Menu/Thames & Hudson

Akhenaten's Egypt
Angela P. Thomas/Shire Publications Ltd

The Pharaohs Master Builders
Henri Stierlin/Terrail

Index

A
Abu Simbel 92,93
Abusir 21
Abydos 9,11,36,37,61
Actium 16
Afghanistan 62,64
Africa 64
Ahmos I 12,90
Akh 26,
Akhenaten (Amenhotep IV)
 13,15,29,38,40,50,65,81,
 86,90,92
Akhet 46
Alexander IV 16
Alexander, The Great 16
Alexandria 16
Amarna Period 38,40,50,
 55,86
Amduat 61
Amenemhat I 11
Amenemope 62
Amenhotep (Amenophis) II
 73,75
Amenhotep III
 29,38,42,76,91–92
Amenhotep IV (Akhenaten)
 13,15,29,38,40,50,65,81,
 86,90,92
Ammit/Ammut 29
Amun 11,13,14,16,34,36,37,
 38,40,42,44,81,90,92,93
Amunherkhepshef 7,78
Amun-Re 37,38,90,92
Amyrtaeus 15
Ankhesenamun 82,85,87
Akhetaten 38,81
Antony, Mark 16,93
Anubis 26,29,31,40–41,86
Anuket 34
Arabs 16,60
Archaic Period 9
Arrhidaeus, Philip 16
Artaxerxes III 15
Assyrians 14,15
Astarte 36
Aswan 21,89,90
Aten 13,38,40,65,81,93
Athribis 14
Atum 34,35,38
Augustus, Emperor 16
Avaris 12
Ay 81,82,87

B
Ba 26,29
Babylonians 15
Bennu 35
Bes 50
Book of the Dead 15,29,67

C
Caesar, Julius 16,92,93
Cairo 23
Cambyses 15
Carnarvon, Lord 81,82,85
Carter, Howard 71,81,82,86
Champollion, Jean-François
 61
Cheops (Khufu) 10,21,23,
 24,89
Chephren 21,24
Christianity 60
Cleopatra VII 16,92–93
Coffin Texts 11,29
Colossi of Memmon 92
Coptic Period 30,62
Coptic script 59,60
Crete 64

D
Dahshur 10,11,21,90
Deir el-Medina 29,76,78
Deir-el-Bahri 54,72,75,90,91
Demotic script 60,61
Djoser 10,18,19,89
Dream Stele 24
Duamutef 32
Duat 29
Dynastic Period 41,59
Dynasty
 1st 9,35
 2nd 60
 3rd 10,19,21,31,35
 4th 10,11,13,21,24,29,30,
 66,89
 5th 9,10,21,55,
 6th 10,19,31,
 7th 10
 8th 10
 9th 10,
 10th 10,
 11th 10,11,13,89,
 12th 11,19,26,29,90
 13th 11
 14th 11
 15th 12,36
 16th 12
 17th 12,37
 18th 12,13,14,15,24,31,37
 38,55,59,62,64,67,72,73
 75,76,78,82,87,90–92
 19th 12,13,15,55,59,73,78
 91,92,93
 20th 12,13,14,73,75
 21st 13,14,25,32,33
 22nd 14,33
 23rd 14
 24th 14
 25th 14,53,64
 26th 14,60
 27th 15
 28th 15
 30th 14
 Macedonian 16
 Saite 14

E
Early Dynastic Period 9,42,
 55,61,88–89
Elephantine 34,37
El-Tarif 72
Enneads 34,35,41

F
First Intermediate Period 10,
 29,36,59,72,76,89,90,92

G
Geb 35,41
Gempaaten 38
Giza 10,11,19,21,23,24,
 35,89
Greco-Roman period 16,56,
 59
Greece 15,16
Greek 61
Greeks 15,16,59,60,62,90
Great Hypostyle Hall 44

H
Hapu 92
Hapy 32
Hathor 7,41,50,73
Hatshepsut 78,90–91
Hattusili 92
Heliopolis 34,35,36,38,41
Heracleopolis 10
Herakhty 38
Hermopolis 34,35,37
Hery seshta 31
hieratic script 9,60
hieroglyphics 9,59,60,61
Hittites 13,92
Hor-Aha 9,88
Horemheb 73,75,81,86
Horus 9,24,29,32,35,37,41,
 66,73
Huni 21
Hyksos 11,12,36–37,62,68,
 72,90

I
Ibis 26
Ibu 31
Imhotep 10,18,19,21
Imsety 32
Intef (Inyotef) I 72
Intef (Inyotef) II 72
Intef (Inyotef) III 72

Inherkha 29
Intermediate Period 29,36,60
Isis 7,26,35,41,50,59
Islam 16,60
Itjtawy 11
Iuput 14

K
Ka 26,32,45
Kadesh 92
Karnak 11,13,36,38,42,44,
 45,90,91,93
Kemet 46
Khafra/e 10,21,23,24,89
Khaemwese (Khaemwaset)
 78
Khepri 38
Kheti 10
Khnum 34,42,50
Khonsu 34,37,44
Khufu (Cheops) 10,21,23,
 24,89
Kiya 81

L
Late Dynastic Period 14–15,
 30,60,64,75
Lebanon 64
Libyans 13,14
Loret, Victor 75
Lower Egypt 9,88,90
Luxor 42,45,93

M
Maat 28,29,35,66,88
Macedonia 16
Manetho 9,88,90
Maspero, Gaston 82
mastaba 9,10.13,19,21
Medjay 66
Meketre 54
Meidum 13
Memphis
 9,10,12,14,18,19,34,35,
 36,81,90
Menes 9,88
Menkaure 10,21,23,24,89
Menna 46
Menthu 37
Mentuhotep I 10,72,
 89–90,92
Mentuhotep II 13,89,90
Mentuhotep IV 11
Merneptah 73
Mesopotamian 9
Middle East 68
Middle Egypt 10
Middle Kingdom 11,12,19,
 29,36,38,42,44,55,59,62,
 68,72,90,92
Montet, Pierre 33
Montu 42
Mortuary Temples 45
Mummification 31–33
Mur 22

Mut 34,37,44
Mycerinus 21

N
Nagada culture 9
Nakhthoreb (Nectanebo II) 15,88
Nakht 67
Nakt 47
Narmer 9,88–89
Nebamun 53,64,73,79
Nebiry 29
Nectanebo II (Nakhthoreb) 15,88
Neferikare 21
Nefermaat 13
Nefertari 36,73,78–79
Nefertiti 15,36,38,40,50, 78,81
Nefertum 34,35
Nekau 14
Nemes 24
Nephthys 35,40
New Kingdom 12–13,30,32, 37,41,44,45,55,56,59,62, 64,65,66,67,68,71,72,75, 76,81,82,88,90
Newbury, Percy 86
Niankhpepi 31
Nile 7,9,21,22,24,29,30,32, 42,45,46,47,53,62,72,92
Nile Delta 9,11,12,14,24,33, 36,61,68
Nile Valley 9,10,61
Ninevah 14
Nubia 11,68,89,90,91,93
Nubian 14,66,69,92
Nut 34,35,41
Nun 35

O
Octavian 16,93
Ogdoads 34,37
Old Kingdom 10,11,19,22, 24,29,31,34,35,37,45,50, 54,55,59,62,64,67,68,89
Orion 23
Osiris 10,11,26–29,32,35, 36,40,41,78

P
Palestine 90
Panekhmen 65
Pashedu 76
Pepi I 31
Pepi/Peppi II 10
Pere 62
Peret 46
Persians 15,16
Pharaonic era 10
Philae 59
Philip Arrhidaeus 16
Piankhi/Piy 14
Pinudjem II 75
Pompey 16,92
Predynastic Period 9,26,34,55
Protodynastic Period 9,88
Psamtek 14
Psusennes I 33
Psusennes II 14
Ptah 34,35,36
Ptolemaic Period 16,55,64
Ptolemy 16
Ptolemy XII 92
Ptolemy XIII 16,92
Ptolemy XIV 16,92,93
Ptolemy XV Caesarion 16, 92,93
Punt 91
Pyramid Age 10
Pyramids 7,11,18–23,35,71
  Bent 10,21
  Great Pyramid 10,19,21, 24,89
  Meidum 21
  Red 10,21
  Step 18,19,21
Pyramid Texts 10,11,22,29

Q
Qebhsnuef 32
Quibell, James E 76

R
Ramasses I 78
Ramesses II 12,13,44,45,61,78,92,93
Ramesses III 7,12,78
Ramesses VI 85
Ramesses XI 14,75

Ramesses IX 75
Ramessid 13,73
Re 22,24,34,35,37,38,41,78, 90,92
Re-Atum 35,36
Re-Harakhte 35
Re-Herakhty 37,38
Reshep 36,37
Roman Empire 7,16,41
Roman Period 16
Rome 16,41,93
Rosetta Stone 60–61

S
Sahure 21
Sais 14
Saite 15
Saqqara 10,18,19,75,82
Satet 34
Schiaparelli, Ernesto 78
Scythians 15
Second Intermediate Period 12,36,59,69,76,90
Second Persian Period 16
Sekhmet 34,35
Sennedjem 26,48,78
Senusret I 11,29
Senusret III 11,90
Sepi 26
Set 26
Seth 35,37,41
Seti (Sethos) I 13,73,78,92
Setnakhte 73
Shabti 31,32
Shawabti 32
Shemu 46
Sheshonq I 14
Sheshonq II 33
Shu 35
Sinai 62,90
Sinai Peninsula 89
Sirius 31,65
Sitre 78
Smenkhkare 40,81,87
Sneferu 10,21
Sobekneferu, Queen 11
Sothis 31,65
Sphinx, Great 10,24–25
Sumerian 59
Syria 64,92

T
Ta-Set-Neferu 78
Tanis 13,33
Tawaret 50
Tawi 67
Tefnut 35
Thebans 12,72,73,81
Thebes 10,12,13,14,34,36, 37,38,40,64,71,72,75,76, 91,92,93
Third Intermediate Period 13–14,33
Thoth 34
Tiye 29,76,92
Tjuyu 76–78
Tutankhamun 12,13,15,53, 66,69,71,72,75,76,81–87
Tutankhaten 40,81
Tuthmosis I 12,72,76
Tuthmosis II 78
Tuthmosis III 12,13,29,61, 73,90,91
Tuthmosis IV 24
Tuya 92
Twosret (Tawosret) 78

U
Unification of Egypt 9
Upper Egypt 9,10,12,14,35, 37,88,90
Userhet 73

V
Valley of the Kings 12,45,61, 71,72,75,76,78,86
Valley of the Nobles 79
Valley of the Queens 78

Y
Young, Thomas 61
Yuja 76–78

Acknowledgments

All photographs © Werner Forman Archive except the following:

6/7, 10/11, 26, 28, 37, 42(t), 48/9, 61(t) 63, 65(b), 73(b), 74/5, 78, 79(t), 82(b) Dr E. Strouhal

Artifacts photographed at the following institutions:

The Egyptian Museum, Cairo: 8, 9, 15, 27, 31, 32(t), 33, 36(b), 41(t), 39, 50, 51, 54(b), 55(b), 62 66, 68, 69(b), 80, 81, 82, 83, 84/5, 86(t), 86(b), 87 Museum of Fine Arts, Boston: 16 Egyptian Museum, Berlin: 29(b), 54(t) Egyptian Museum, Turin: 14, 29(t), 53(b) British Museum, London 34, 47, 52, 55(t), 61(b), 67 Christie's, London: 35, 57 Royal Museum of Art and History, Brussels: 40 Schimmel Collection, New York: 38 The Louvre, Paris: 56 (and 4), 60 Detroit Institute of Art: 65(t) The Schindler Collection, New York: 92 Daedallus Gallery, New York: 30

The publisher would like to thank
Themis Halvantzi and Barbara Heller at the Werner Forman Archive,
and Jane Benn for their help in producing this book.